SHADOW WORK ORACLE WORKBOOK

MYSTICAL PROMPTS & EMPOWERING EXERCISES TO ILLUMINATE YOUR SECRET DARKNESS & UNITE YOUR SOUL

NIKKI GOLDSTEIN

Go2Guru
PUBLISHING

ISBN
Hardcover: 978-1-923162-16-7
Paperback: 978-1-923162-17-4
E-Book: 978-1-923162-18-1
Cover design by Tika Design
Interior Formatting by Publishing Services
Publisher: Go2Guru Publishing www.go2gurupublishing.com

Disclaimer

The information provided in this book is designed to provide helpful information on the subjects discussed. The author's books only provide the reader with basic knowledge of specific topics without any guarantees concerning results. This book is for educational and entertainment purposes only. While the utmost care has been taken in compiling the information in this book, and every effort has been made to ensure the contents are accurate, up-to-date, reliable and complete. **It must not be treated as a substitute for qualified medical advice, including psychological advice.** No warranties of any kind are declared or implied. Readers acknowledge that the author does not render legal, financial, professional or medical advice. Always consult a qualified medical practitioner. Neither the Author nor the Publisher can be held responsible for any loss or claim arising from the use or misuse of the suggestions made or the failure to take medical advice. Consult your physician before beginning any diet, exercise or psychological program or practices.

TABLE OF CONTENTS

Dedication – To Aurora, my sister-soul, who taught me to write and has held my hand along the dark by-ways of the soul for infinite lifetimes.

NIKKI'S STORY - UNVEILING THE AUTHENTIC ME

I was about 12 years old when I first recognised that I was different. For years, my sister and I had played a game where I'd get Georgie to hold a coloured jack in her hand, I'd hover my palm above her closed fist, and I'd guess the colour. Georgie was a couple of years younger than me, and she thought it was a great lark that I'd guess right most of the time.

Then, for Christmas after my 12th birthday, my mom gave me my first deck of tarot cards. The deck was the Aquarian Tarot by David Palladini, and they fascinated me. A pictorial masterpiece of art-deco imagery blended with medieval tarot symbolism, they were so beautiful that I couldn't wait to play with them.

My family and I went to a friend's party a few days after Christmas. I thought it would be fun to read everyone's fortunes, so I took the cards with me. We had lots of laughs interpreting the spreads and reading up on the Minor and Major Arcana meanings. That day, I did a reading for a beautiful girl called Catherine, and that reading changed my life.

Catherine was a talented ballerina. She'd won a scholarship to dance in a prestigious European ballet company. I saw many ominous cards in her spread, and a thought popped into my mind to warn her to look after her ankles. I don't know why that thought occurred; it wasn't explicit in the cards. No sign spelled out that she was in danger of an injury; there were no Swords or Death or Hanged Man cards in the spread, but it was nevertheless what I felt prompted to say to her.

Some months later, my mother got off the phone from Catherine's mom, and she looked as white as a sheet. Catherine had had a terrible accident. She slipped off the stage in Monaco and broke both her ankles. The breaks were so bad they ended her ballet career.

Everyone remembered what I'd told her that day at the family barbeque. I felt a mixture of horror, shame and terror at my prediction. I wrapped up the cards and buried them at the back of my wardrobe. Not only did I shun the cards, I banished that side of myself to the deepest, darkest part of being.

But you can't unknow what you know. I knew something mysterious, ineffable, and ungraspable moved through me when I played the Jacks game with Georgie and did the reading for Catherine. I was "called" by something within myself that seemed frightening, dark, and malevolent. If it was part of me, I didn't want to know about it.

Years passed, and I forgot about the cards in my wardrobe. I also forgot about the part of me that liked to play psychic games as a child.

At 21, I went to live in the UK. To this day, I don't know why, but I dug the tarot deck out of the cupboard, wrapped it in a pink silk sari a friend had given me, and dropped it into my suitcase to take with me to London.

When I arrived, I quickly got a job in fashion, and for the first few months, I had a ball–going to nightclubs, meeting the rich and famous and working as a stylist for some of the most recognisable brands in the world. I was dreadfully, pitifully poor, but I didn't care! I was having such a good time.

I'd been living in a friend's flat rent-free, but she decided to go off and live in LA, which meant I had to find enough cash to rent somewhere else. Another friend, who knew I had an interest in the tarot, offered me a job doing readings at his homeopathy clinic. Desperate for money, I agreed, and the next week, I had a full slate of appointments for readings lined up.

At first, I was scared witless. What if I saw terrible things in the cards? Death? Accidents? Breakups? Loss? I feared the darkness, not just in people's lives, but what I might uncover in myself.

One day, I did a reading for Jenny, a wise older lady. She said to me, "You're good at this, but you'll be even better when you accept this spooky part of yourself". I was taken aback by what she'd seen in me. I was doing everything in my power to keep this part of myself suppressed, tucked in and a secret.

Jenny suggested I make an appointment with a woman she knew who was high up in one of the psychic associations of Great Britain. If you're investigating the mystical side of yourself, the UK is the place to do it–the place is crawling with mediums, psychics, healers, witches, Wiccans, Druids and every other practitioner of the magic arts you can imagine.

Joan looked like any ordinary granny. She was close to 80 years old but had a twinkle in her eye and a spring in her step. She invited me to sit and have a cup of tea. We sat at her dining room table in the most ordinary dining room in the world and chatted about the weather and the woeful state of the London transport system, and then, suddenly, she transformed. The benign granny became a beacon of power and energy. She turned to me and said, "What use are you to yourself or anyone else if you shrink from who you really are?" I hadn't said a word about why I was there; she just knew I was a young woman seeking advice who was a friend of a friend.

Her gaze was so penetrating and intense that she almost blew off the top of my head. I sat back in the chair, reeling. "You have a gift, but you'll never be able to use it to its full effect until you embrace it. You must accept who you are and stop running. If you don't, one day you'll run into a brick wall or worse".

With surprising firmness, she grabbed my arm and ushered me to the door. I'd hardly finished my tea! I had so many questions, but it was clear she'd said her piece, and she wasn't going to say any more.

I called Jenny and told her what had happened, and she just laughed. She laughed at my youth, my naivete, and my lack of wisdom.

But I took Joan's words to heart and started actively doing the work needed to integrate. Shadow Work.

I read Jung widely, the father of analytic psychology, as well as Robert A. Johnson, a Jungian who wrote the book "Owning Your Own Shadow". I also read "Women Who Run With The Wolves" by Clarissa Pinkola Estes, an American writer and Jungian psychoanalyst, which literally turned my head upside down and transformed life.

Pinkola Estes uses myths and fairy tales to explain psychic states. I experienced the book as a personal awakening to other realms. I remember reading her interpretation of the Hans Christian Andersen classic "The Red Shoes" about a girl who can't stop dancing. The red shoes are so seductive that they enslave her. In Pinkola Estes's version, the red shoes represent the wild psyche, an aspect of ourselves that society often seeks to control and suppress, and which is often banished to the Shadow's realm. She says we need to appreciate it, defend it and be careful not to hand over its wild power. But the Red Shoes is also a cautionary tale. It reminds us not to get so caught up in the powers of our wild natures that we're swept off our feet and become ungrounded. I realised that a large part of my fear of my secret self was the very uncontrollability, uncontainability and fury of its true nature. I was afraid to come unfastened from my moorings and lose touch with the conventional world.

As I worked in the clinic doing readings, I became more comfortable with my abilities. I gradually accepted my fears surrounding this mysterious power and worked to ground myself and bring the darkness into the light.

What I belated realised is that my dark side not only contained my psychic powers but also housed my creativity, my rebelliousness, my black sense of humour and my sexuality. None of these traits was particularly celebrated in women at that time, and it took me many years to integrate and rejoice in them.

As an older woman, I love the fact that these days I give zero fucks what other people think of me. I laugh loudly at inappropriate jokes. I relish the opportunity I get to do readings for friends and occasional clients, and I wear what I want, say what I want and do what I want (if it does no harm to anyone else).

None of this could have been accomplished without accepting and embracing my Shadow. But I'm not going to gild the lily: Shadow Work is not for the faint-hearted. It takes guts and determination to excavate the part of ourselves we'd rather leave hidden. Bringing whatever lurks in the shadows into the full light of day can be a daunting and sometimes disabling task–especially if there's trauma involved.

Hiding our wild selves is often a survival tactic. In families and cultures that are controlling, repressive, highly codified and religious, being who you really are can be a dangerous exercise. Women are maimed and killed in many places in the world for going against the status quo. And whilst men are not the enemy, the patriarchy isn't fond of powerful women who speak their truth and stomp on the rules. Sometimes, you need a suit of armour for this journey.

This book is dedicated to safely and wisely excavating the Shadow. I haven't plucked the exercises in this Workbook from nowhere; they're based on tried-and-tested therapeutic practices. I've used most of them in my spiritual practice for years. I've studied counselling and done three years of intense coursework in Jungian philosophy.

Doing "The Work" gives you the tools you need to navigate this path with certainty and wisdom. I was lucky to meet incredible people on my journey to wholeness, but I wish there were resources like this when I was a young girl looking for clues to who I really was.

I'm writing this Workbook for all the wild ones, dreamers, would-be magicians, maverick and shadow-creepers out there seeking truth. You may have a sense that a part of you is missing, dormant, passive or mute–I'm going to help you bring that spirit to life!

If you're a little bit afraid of your dark side, that's completely normal. By the time you've finished this Workbook, you'll want to throw a party and introduce her/him/them to the world. Unifying the dark and light sides of yourself releases so much freedom, power, energy, and, most importantly, self-love and self-acceptance.

> *"I am a broken person. And I know exactly where my cracks are and how deep they run. I don't pretend to not be a broken person and therein lies the big difference. Because the truth is, we are all broken in places, but it is those who know exactly where and how they are broken, who also know exactly where and how they are whole! And we may not be whole in all places and in all ways, but we take whatever wholeness that we do have, and we make good of it. And we try hard to work on the broken parts, and we ask for help when we need it."*
>
> — C. JOYBELL C.

As I mentioned above, I spent three years studying Jungian psychology. I'm by no means an expert, but I discovered a passion for Jungian ideas that has fuelled and fed my life. I've been working with a Jungian analyst for many years–because a wise guide is always an asset for the often-challenging task of excavating the Shadow. Shadow Work is the surest path I know to self-love. No doubt it will bring its own share of challenges and, at times, misgivings and doubts, but I know from my travels on the dark side that this is one of the most rewarding and empowering journeys you'll ever take.

May all your dark dreams, nightmares, shame-filled regrets and self-loathing find their place in the sun so you can embrace it all and become whole.

I'll be here every step to light the way for you.

Nikki xx

WHY WORK WITH YOUR SHADOW?

We don't need a technical term to know what our Shadow is. It's the part of ourselves we want to hide from the rest of the world and, often, ourselves, too. It's usually the aspect that causes us fear, disgust or self-loathing. For many of us, it's so revolting and shame-inducing that we shove it deep down inside ourselves—sometimes never to see the light of day again.

It's the Shadow that feels and expresses jealousy, pride, greed, anger, superiority, inferiority, insincerity, moodiness, gluttony, laziness, and so on. We don't have to look far to see it in action.

I'll set the scene: a mother leaves her five-year-old daughter playing happily with her two-year-old brother. As soon as her back is turned, the five-year-old grabs the boy's toy and pushes him over to get what she wants. Mom returns to find the two-year-old in tears and her daughter looking smug and triumphant. That's the Shadow in full flight.

Scene two: the mother, ashamed of her daughter's cruelty and determined to improve her behaviour, scolds her, "Ivy, you naughty girl! Give your brother his toy and don't do that again!".

Scene three: the daughter, realising her mother disapproves of her triumph in wresting the toy from her annoying little brother (who usually gets the lion's share of her mother's attention), quickly realises (though this insight would be so lightning-fast, silent and stealthy that it evades the conscious mind) this behaviour is not acceptable and drives her need to dominate and steal from her brother underground.

This scenario is a classic Shadow play.

In this imagined minor family drama, the girl grows up resenting and competing with her brother. But because her mother loves and approves of her when she's a "good girl", she hides these feelings of inferiority and shame and pretends to love her brother–the cuckoo in her nest.

So, what would it take for Ivy to let go of these dark feelings?

It's not as hard as you'd imagine. It would only take a shift in her awareness about where all those negative feelings towards her brother were concealed inside her. Maybe she realises there's something wrong when she rows often with a co-worker (who coincidentally reminds her of her brother)? Or maybe she wakes up one day, feeling the dreadful heaviness in her heart for a sibling relationship that has never fully functioned, and grieves this sadness with a palpable ache? Whatever the motivating factor, an urge inside Ivy to become whole brings her to Shadow Work.

But it's not just on the micro-level that we see the Shadow expressing itself. The Shadow exerts an influence on the collective, too. The Nazi movement in Germany during the 1930s up to the end of WWII was a mass expression of the Shadow. The wars in the Middle East today are a terrible outpouring of the Shadow. The partisanship we see in politics, the environmental neglect, racism and social discord, which are hallmarks of 21st-century life, are all examples of when our personal Shadows identify, blend and buy into the dark forces in our society.

We only need to glance at social media to clock the hatred and anger expressed by key-board warriors. Protected by the four walls of their homes and the anonymity afforded by their avatars, they allow their Shadows to launch forth in vitriolic outrage at differing political opinions or lash out because they think they've been ripped off, victimised, ghosted, maligned or marginalised–you name the slight there will be someone, or many people, who take offence. All this anger and fury is the Shadow with the guard rails down.

No one on earth is all sweetness, light, rainbows, and puppy dogs all the time. We all have a Shadow side, which exerts tremendous power over our lives.

There are no exact measurements of how much of our psyche is taken up with the Shadow. Still, according to Carl Jung, the father of Shadow Work, it's any part of ourselves we perceive as inferior, evil or unacceptable. He believed we ***repress*** this aspect to make ourselves palatable and pleasing to others and ourselves.

I'll tell you a story about Sarah. She came to me for a tarot reading some years ago and was going through a period of intense self-analysis because she'd bounced from one bad relationship to another. She craved a steady, loving, compassionate relationship with a man but seemed not to attract them.

What she discovered through the reading and the Shadow Work she did after that session was that it wasn't the men who didn't want to stick with her–in fact, it was the complete opposite; it was *her* lack of availability that made them feel inferior, bitter, and rejected. In Jung's terms, she'd ***projected*** her feelings of worthlessness onto the men she was pursuing. The men weren't rejecting her; she was rejecting them! She just couldn't see it for what it was–then.

This insight didn't deliver the perfect partner overnight. However, it began a journey into the darkest corners of her psyche, where she discovered that her fear of intimacy sprang from a deep fear that she was profoundly unworthy and not good enough to attract the love she desired. It's a much longer story, but Sarah had become an expert in unavailability, supremely self-protective, outwardly confident but inwardly self-loathing. Paradoxically, she'd become an artful model of her very emotionally unavailable work-addicted Dad.

It took work, courage, and an unstinting commitment to excavate the parts of herself that were deeply hidden (sometimes so deeply hidden that it took many attempts and years to unearth them), but eventually, with persistence and self-belief she was able to bring them into the light.

Sarah has been happily married with two kids and a dog for ten years. Her work on integrating her Shadow-Self with her Light-Self also improved her relationship with her father. "I'd been irrationally angry with him since I was a kid. I was bitterly disappointed that he never seemed to have time for me. When I finally gave up being mad at him, I saw that he was just as wounded from his childhood as I was from mine, and I developed compassion for him that opened our relationship in a way that seemed impossible before".

The Swiss psychiatrist and psychoanalyst Carl Jung believed that the Shadow is the repository of all our darkness, but that's not the whole picture. He also thought the Shadow held the keys to enormous power. Here's the irony and the mystery: if we're brave enough to enter the Shadow-realm, we also get the keys to the kingdom. Concealed within the Shadow is the tremendous power and potential of your creativity, humour, fury, sensuality, sexuality, self-acceptance, self-love, and universal love too. It seems obvious, but when we can love and accept ourselves unconditionally, we're much better at loving and accepting others unconditionally.

The Shadow is the threshold we all must cross to become whole. If we cut ourselves off from our Shadow, we're not only limiting access to our power, but we're living half-lives. When we integrate the Shadow, instead of repressing it or shaming it out of sight, we're opening a doorway to more energy, life force, self-love, creativity and vitality–unlimited powers we could never have imagined.

CHAPTER ONE

MEETING THE SHADOW

Ready to begin a transformative journey into the depths of your inner world? In the following pages, we'll lift the veils of the unconscious to reveal the unexplored territories of the Shadow. This exploration is not just an act of courage; it's a profound commitment to

personal growth, a dance with the unknown parts of ourselves that we've long neglected or concealed.

This chapter delves into Shadow Work, a concept originating from Carl Jung's insightful mind. Shadow work encourages us to embrace every aspect of our being–the light and the dark, the known and the unknown. It challenges us to confront our hidden fears, secret desires, and suppressed emotions, transforming them into sources of strength, light, self-love, and self-awareness.

Prepare to meet your inner Oracle–your secret superpower. Often hidden in the deep recesses of the Shadow and known more parochially as your intuition, this mystical faculty, which each of us is given at birth, can be harnessed to transform you into the high priestess or priest of your deepest soul. With direct transmissions from your Oracle at your fingertips, you grow in power, resilience and insight.

Anticipate being captivated by your psyche's quirks and complexities. Be ready to encounter exercises and reflections that will enlighten you and stir your soul. This is a restart in life—where you meet, embrace, and integrate your Shadow, emerging more enlightened, whole, and truly alive.

I've called this book the Shadow Work Oracle because an Oracle is two things at once: in ancient Greece, it was a priestess or priest who operated as a ***medium*** through which prophecies would be channelled. But an Oracle is also ***the message*** that is channelled. And that message is usually deemed wise, authoritative, mystical, wise, prescriptive and profound.

So, why is this important in the context of Shadow Work?

The easy answer is that *I want to empower you to become the priest or priestess, shaman, mystic and healer of your own life.* And I want to encourage you to travel to the dark realms of your psyche with a tour guide (this very Journal you're gripping right now!) and return with the wisdom you need to channel the sacred messages for yourself.

As you progress through this Workbook, ***you will become the Oracle.***

Many of the exercises, prompts, and affirmations are based on Jungian concepts of the Shadow. They are part of a rich tradition of psychoanalysis that has been practiced since the 1940s, when, in 1945, Jung gave his clear-cut definition of the Shadow as "The thing a person has no wish to be". But it's not just Jungian ideas in this book: I've brought together many therapeutic strands that deal with Dark and Light archetypes. I've tapped into Cognitive Behavior Therapy, Person-Centered Therapy, dream language, tarot wisdom, mindfulness and ancient, universal archetypes, and Jung's work on the Shadow, to provide insights into the human psyche. This very personal book is about what's worked for me, mostly through trial and error, and brought together in one easy-to-understand-and-use compendium.

For a while now, Jung has been out of fashion, and faster, more solution-oriented therapies such as Cognitive Behaviour Therapy and Solutions-Focused Therapy have become more the vogue for treating mental illness and psychological distress. However, we can't talk about the Shadow or investigate Shadow Work without acknowledging and celebrating its origins.

In its day, Jung's concept of the Shadow caused a sensation in the worlds of psychotherapy and mental health. Many therapists became instant fans, but just as quickly, many eschewed his philosophies–some thought he was a magician, and others thought he was a madman.

This chapter is your gateway to understanding the profound concept of the Shadow, a term first coined by Carl Jung and further explored by analysts such as Robert A. Johnson, Marie-Louise von Franz, James Hillman and Marion Woodman. The Shadow isn't just a mere psychological term; it's a vital and powerful part of our psyche that affects our relationships, health, energy, work and even the choices we make in life.

> *"One does not become enlightened by imagining figures of light, but by making the darkness conscious. The latter procedure, however, is disagreeable and therefore not popular."*
>
> — C.G. JUNG

But why should you care about the Shadow? Well, embracing your Shadow is critical to personal growth and self-awareness. In this chapter, we'll explore where you are on your path to discovering and owning your Shadow, and you'll do a writing exercise to investigate your first encounter with your Shadow-Self.

Before we deep-dive, a few key concepts are valuable to understand as you step through this Workbook. Jung was interested in the mysteries of life. He saw parallels between the search for spiritual gold, that is, the integration of the light and dark sides of the personality, and the medieval alchemists' search for physical gold, where, bent over alembics, beakers and burners in hidden attics, they aimed to transform base metals such as lead and mercury into physical gold. On the surface, it looked like the alchemists were looking to find riches by transforming iron, copper and tin into gold. But, in truth, their search was spiritual, metaphysical, symbolic and metaphorical as much as it was physical. The base metals represented the dark elements of the soul and psyche, whereas gold represented what they believed was the highest pursuit of human existence–to find *en-**light**-en-ment*. In short, gold equalled transcendence, merging the human soul with the divine soul to create a unified being.

THE FOUR STAGES TOWARDS WHOLENESS AND ENLIGHTENMENT

Jung often used the metaphor of alchemy to explain his concept of ***individuation.*** Individuation is the process of integrating different aspects of the psyche to achieve self-realization and wholeness, in simple terms, integrating the light with the dark. Jung drew parallels between this process and the stages of the alchemical Magnum Opus, or "Great Work," which aimed at the spiritual transformation of the alchemist's soul from unenlightened to enlightened.

The four primary stages of the Magnum Opus in alchemy, which Jung equated with stages of psychological development, are **Nigredo, Albedo, Citrinitas**, and **Rubedo.**

Nigredo (Blackening): This stage represents confrontation with the Shadow, the dark and unconscious part of the psyche. It's a period of disintegration, where old beliefs and illusions are broken down. This often corresponds with experiences of depression, chaos, or existential crisis, where the individual must face their inner darkness and previously unconscious material.

Albedo (Whitening): In this stage, the individual explores and integrates the unconscious. It's associated with purification and gaining clarity. This stage often involves encountering the ***anima*** or ***animus*** (the opposite gender aspects within the psyche, i.e. the masculine and feminine traits we have whether we're born male or female or even gender non-binary), leading to a greater understanding of oneself and the unconscious forces at work. It's a phase of self-discovery and enlightenment.

Citrinitas (Yellowing): Traditionally, this stage is seen as a step towards enlightenment and the dawning of "solar consciousness," or awakening to who you are like a metaphorical sun rising. Citrinitas represents the development of wisdom. In psychological terms, this stage involves further integrating the unconscious into consciousness and deepening understanding. It's often associated with the development of intuition and a more profound sense of self.

Rubedo (Reddening): This final stage signifies the achievement of wholeness and the harmonious integration of the conscious and unconscious aspects of the self. It represents self-realization, individuation, and a rebirth of the personality. The individual achieves a balance between opposites (e.g., masculine and feminine, dark and light) within themselves.

Jung's interpretation of alchemy as a metaphor for psychological development provided a framework for understanding the ***distinct stages of psychological wholeness or individuation***.

Let's see where you're at in your alchemical journey to ***individuation.*** Do this quiz to gain insights and pointers about your next steps.

QUIZ - DISCOVER YOUR STAGE IN THE JOURNEY TO INDIVIDUATION

Instructions: Answer each question with "Never", "Rarely", "Sometimes", "Often", or "Always".

- Do you find yourself contemplating the deeper meaning of life's challenges?
- Do you feel overwhelmed by your emotions or thoughts?
- Do you recognize repetitive patterns in your behavior that you wish to change?
- Are you comfortable acknowledging your flaws and weaknesses?
- Do you often feel misunderstood by those around you?
- Do you actively seek to understand your dreams and unconscious thoughts?
- Have you had moments of significant self-realization or enlightenment?
- Do you feel a sense of clarity about who you truly are?
- Do you regularly engage in self-reflection or meditation?
- Are you able to acknowledge and integrate conflicting aspects of your personality?
- Do you feel a strong connection to your intuition or inner wisdom?
- Do you find it easy to adapt to new insights about yourself?
- Do you often experience a sense of personal growth and development?
- Do you feel a sense of wholeness or unity within yourself?
- Are you often aware of the underlying motives of your actions?
- Do you feel that you have a balanced understanding of your masculine and feminine traits?
- How often do you feel a sense of inner peace and contentment?
- Do you find that you can easily express your true self to others?

- Do you feel connected to a higher purpose or a greater sense of meaning in life?
- Are you able to find harmony in your relationships and interactions with others?
- Do you feel that you have overcome significant personal obstacles or traumas?
- Do you see your life experiences as opportunities for learning and growth?
- Do you feel that you are living authentically, in line with your true self?
- Do you often feel a sense of joy and fulfillment in your daily life?

Scoring

Never: 1 point
Rarely: 2 points
Sometimes: 3 points
Often: 4 points
Always: 5 points

Results

24-48 Points - Nigredo: You are in the initial stage of self-discovery, possibly facing personal darkness, confusion, or emotional upheaval. It's important to confront and explore these feelings. Consider seeking therapy or journaling to process these emotions.

49-72 Points - Albedo: You are in the process of understanding and integrating the unconscious to become whole. Focus on mindfulness practices, dream analysis, and creative expression to further this journey.

73-96 Points - Citrinitas: You have achieved a level of wisdom and are developing your inner knowledge. Continue to hone your intuition and use your insights for personal growth and helping others.

97-120 Points - Rubedo: You are in the advanced stage of individuation, experiencing a sense of wholeness, unification and balance. Maintain this through ongoing self-reflection, spiritual practices, and engaging in activities that align with your true self.

Advice for Advancement

From Nigredo to Albedo: Embrace self-reflection. Seek to understand the root causes of your emotions and behaviors. Therapy or guided meditation can be beneficial.

From Albedo to Citrinitas: Deepen your self-awareness. Engage in activities that nurture your intuition and wisdom, such as meditation, reading, and meaningful conversations.

From Citrinitas to Rubedo: Focus on living authentically and aligning your actions with your inner wisdom. Practice mindfulness and continue to cultivate balance in all areas of your life.

This quiz is a reflective tool and not a definitive measure. It's designed to help you consider where you are on your path to connecting to your Shadow.

Engaging with these exercises is your first step to seeing yourself fully, without filters, and learning to embrace all parts of your being. The journey towards understanding your Shadow is not about eliminating these hidden aspects of your personality (we can't get rid of them even if we try) but about accepting and integrating them into your whole self and loving yourself, not despite them–but because of them.

> *"A life truly lived constantly burns away veils of illusion, burns away what is no longer relevant, gradually reveals our essence, until, at last, we are strong enough to stand in our naked truth. Instead of transcending ourselves, we must move into ourselves."*
>
> — MARION WOODMAN

JUNG'S CONCEPT OF THE EGO AND THE SHADOW

According to Carl Jung's analytical psychology, the ego represents the conscious mind, the center of our identity and our sense of self. It's the part of our psyche that we typically identify with in our everyday lives. The ego is responsible for our rational thoughts, decision-making, and our interactions with the external world. The ego lives in the light.

On the other hand, The Shadow is the unconscious aspect of our personality. As I've begun to outline, it comprises all the elements of ourselves that we repress, deny, or ignore because they don't fit our self-image or societal norms. These can be negative traits, desires, fears, or impulses that we find threatening to our ego and they often remain in the Dark.

The relationship between the ego and the Shadow is complex and often fraught with tension. The ego strives to maintain a sense of control and order, often by suppressing or ignoring aspects of the Shadow. However, the Shadow doesn't disappear; it lurks in the depths of our unconscious, influencing our thoughts, emotions, and behaviors in subtle ways.

Jung believed that embracing and integrating the Shadow is essential for personal growth and individuation. In Jungian therapy, the process of individuation involves confronting the Shadow and integrating its contents into consciousness. This is achieved not by crushing the ego or suppressing the Shadow, but by giving ourselves gentle, loving kindness. Ideally, these energies can't be forced into submission just because we will it, but in time, coaxed lovingly, beckoned gracefully and shaped into a more whole and unified person.

Now that you've done the quiz and familiarised yourself with the terms "ego" "Shadow" and "individuation", the next step is to set aside some time for this simple yet profound writing exercise. It invites you to recall your first encounter with your Shadow. This could be a moment when you felt a sudden surge of emotion that seemed foreign or when you acted in a way that felt out of character. These moments are gateways to understanding your Shadow.

JOURNALING YOUR FIRST ENCOUNTER WITH THE SHADOW

Objective

To explore and reflect on your initial encounter with the Shadow aspect of your personality.

How To Do It

Step 1.

Find a quiet and comfortable space

Where you won't be disturbed. Make sure you have enough time to engage with this exercise without rushing.

Step 2.

Relax and Reflect

Spend a few minutes in relaxation, perhaps with deep breathing or meditation, to clear your mind and focus inward.

Step 3.

Recall the Encounter

Think back to a moment in your life when you experienced a strong emotional reaction, conflict, or a realization that felt uncomfortable or surprising. This could be an event where you acted out of character, had an unexpected emotional outburst, or encountered a part of yourself you didn't know existed.

Step 4.

Start Writing

Using the writing prompts below, begin to write about this experience. Don't worry about grammar or structure; focus on expressing your thoughts and feelings as freely as possible.

Step 5.

Reflect

After writing, spend some time reflecting on what you have written. Consider what insights you have gained about your Shadow and how this encounter has influenced your personal growth.

Writing Prompts

- Describe the situation or event that led to your encounter with the Shadow.
- What was happening, and who was involved?

- Explore your feelings and thoughts during this encounter. What emotions surfaced?
- Did any of these feelings surprise you?
- Reflect on any physical sensations you experienced. Did your body react a certain way (e.g., tension, adrenaline rush, stomach knots)?
- Analyse your behavior during this encounter. How did you act, and how did this differ from your usual behavior?
- Consider the aftermath of this encounter. How did you feel immediately after? Were there any long-term effects on your thoughts or behaviors?
- Consider what this encounter revealed about your hidden desires, fears, or unresolved issues.
- Contemplate how this experience has influenced your understanding of yourself. Have you noticed any changes in your attitude or perspective since this encounter?

Note

It's important to approach this exercise with an open mind and a non-judgmental attitude towards yourself. Encounters with the Shadow can be challenging. If you find this exercise brings up intense emotions, consider discussing your reflections with a therapist or a person you trust.

Now that you've got a few of these concepts under your belt, it's time to discover more about how to recognise your Shadow and how to call it out when it's wreaking havoc in your life (which it's wont to do when it's left lurking in the darkness). You're about to be armed with an array of tools to help you flush your dark side out of its hiding places and allow it the freedom to express itself more fully in your life.

Shadow Chronicle – John's Story

"I was the classic shy kid. I liked playing computer games and reading, and I used to submerge myself in those worlds because I really didn't like who I was. I felt awkward and unpopular and struggled to find friends. When I was a teenager and starting to go to parties, I found that alcohol emboldened me. Instead of being the shy guy, I felt unbeatable and confident. It wasn't long before I was drinking before school, too – a little shot in the morning to give my ego a lift. By the time I got to college, I was a full-blown convert alcoholic. Unfortunately, I was good at holding my booze, so no one noticed I was flying a lot of the time. I wasn't a messy drunk. Then I met Sam, the person I credit for saving my life. He saw traits in me he had in himself–suppressed darkness, low confidence and an alcohol dependence. After a lot of convincing, Sam got me to a drug and alcohol counsellor, and that lady introduced me to the idea that I was in pain and running from my true self. Since then, I've read a lot about the Shadow and I do the work. It's hard, and I have to admit that I will have to work on my addictions for the rest of my life, but if it wasn't for Sam and his courage to tell me the truth about who I was being, I might not be here today".

MANIFESTATION IN LIFE AND EMOTIONS

The Shadow often manifests as unexplained mood swings, intense emotional reactions, or feelings of emptiness. You might overreact to minor issues or feel angry, jealous, or insecure. These emotional outbursts are Shadow's way of signalling unresolved issues or repressed emotions. Another common manifestation is ***projection***, where we attribute our own unacceptable qualities to others. For example, frequently criticising others for being lazy or dishonest might reflect your unacknowledged tendencies.

Physical Manifestations

The Shadow can manifest physically in the body, often through symptoms like chronic tension, fatigue, or psychosomatic illnesses. These physical manifestations can be your body's way of expressing unresolved emotional turmoil. For instance, a constantly stiff neck might symbolise the heavy burden of unspoken words or repressed anger.

In the Workplace

In your professional life, the Shadow might appear as recurring conflicts with colleagues, feelings of inadequacy, or a tendency to undermine your successes. It can also show up as envy towards others' achievements or an irrational fear of failure. These patterns often stem from deeper insecurities or subconscious beliefs about not being good enough.

In Relationships

In relationships, the Shadow can be seen in the repeated repulsion or attraction to certain types of people, often leading to dysfunctional dynamics. It might also manifest as a tendency to sabotage relationships or an irrational fear of intimacy. These patterns can be traced back to unresolved issues from past experiences, such as childhood trauma or past relationship wounds. The Shadow loves harboring old resentments, holding onto past trauma and playing the victim.

Emotional Triggers

Notice situations where your emotional response seems disproportionate. These are clues to underlying Shadow aspects.

Repetitive Patterns

Look for recurring themes in your life problems, whether in relationships, work, or personal behavior. These patterns often point to Shadow elements at play.

Body Signals

Be aware of physical symptoms that don't have a clear medical explanation, such as aches and pains that are not attributed to diagnosed conditions or signs of tension and stress in the body. These could be manifestations of psychological and Shadow conflicts. Note: If you have any persistent health challenges, seek professional medical advice.

Addictions

Whether you're addicted to work, gambling, food, alcohol or some other substance abuse problems, these patterns, which are seemingly hard to relinquish, can be signs of the Shadow at play in your life. If you have issues in these areas, seek professional medical advice. And a caveat–the Shadow hates being flushed out of the places where addictions have a hold on you; anger, denial, and wilful ignorance are all ways the Shadow will tell you that you don't have a problem. Search your soul more deeply to discover where additions may conceal themselves.

Dramas

If you often find yourself trapped like a hamster on a wheel of drama, you may be in the grip of Shadow play. Persistent relationship problems and regular dramatic scenes can be places to begin your search for the Shadow at work in your life. Gossiping, spreading rumours and innuendo can also be places to look for Shadow influences.

Maladaptive Behaviours

If you engage in self-harming behaviors in any way (and this doesn't have to mean hurting yourself physically), such as being in an abusive relationship, permitting toxic behaviours from friends, family and colleagues, or even excessive self-criticism, may be signs your Shadow has you in its grip. Seek professional advice for strategies for support.

AWARENESS TOOLS FOR SHADOW TRACES

This book is dedicated to giving you all the self-awareness tools you need to flush the Shadow from its hiding place in your deep subconscious and bring it into the light where it can be embraced and integrated. In this book, you'll hear me talk a lot about the following tools to help you track, monitor and illuminate the Shadow.

Journaling

Keeping a journal can help you track your emotional states, thoughts, and reactions, providing insights into your Shadow.

Dream Analysis

Dreams can be a direct window into the unconscious. Pay attention to recurring symbols or themes in your dreams.

Professional Support

Sometimes, others can see aspects of our Shadow more clearly than we can. Open, honest feedback from trusted mentors, coaches, or therapists can be enlightening.

Mindfulness and Meditation

Practices like mindfulness and meditation can help you become more aware of your unconscious thoughts and feelings and help you develop self-love, self-compassion and self-awareness.

We've just touched on some basic Shadow Work concepts to invite you into its world. Right now, you're at the very beginning of your adventure and could consider yourself to be a novice. Yes, you still have training wheels on, but, I promise, that if you do the work with reverence, self-compassion and diligence you will become an initiate into this mysterious realm and, in time, you will become a master of these extraordinary arts. My hope is that one day very soon you will become the Oracle and will have access to all the sacred knowledge you crave. Read on to discover your path.

CHAPTER TWO

RECOGNIZING THE SHADOW

It's time to equip yourself with tools to spot the Shadow and to understand its whispers and roars as it influences your life from the wings. You're about to receive a powerful flashlight designed to illuminate even the darkest corners of your psyche, offering a beacon of insight that transforms ineffable shadows into tangible forms.

This exploration of self-awareness will be as enlightening as it is empowering. You'll learn to identify when your Shadow is playing puppeteer and how you can take back the strings. This is not merely about confronting what you find unsettling or unfamiliar; it's about recognising that each shadowy part of your personality holds untapped potential, power and wisdom.

As we delve into the intricate play of light and dark, you'll discover how to give your Shadow a voice, allowing it to express itself constructively —and transforming you into the Oracle you were always meant to be. By integrating these Shadow aspects, you'll harness a more profound sense of freedom and authenticity. Prepare to be inspired as you step onto a path of fearless self-discovery and embrace the full spectrum of your being.

Recognising your Shadow is like meeting a long-lost friend. You'll be surprised by what you see when you gaze at your reflection for more than a few seconds as you're brushing your hair or cleaning your teeth. The person staring back at you is someone you know well, but perhaps someone you haven't deeply considered before.

The mirror work exercise is a powerful tool. Standing in front of a mirror, looking unflinchingly into your own eyes, you'll confront those pieces of yourself you've avoided. This exercise is not about judgment but acknowledgment, self-compassion and understanding.

By the end of this chapter, you'll have a clearer picture of your personality's secret aspects. This awareness is the foundation of true self-knowledge and personal growth. Recognising your Shadow is a brave act that sets you on the path to self-discovery and liberation from unconscious patterns.

> *"Our shadows hold the essence of who we are. They hold our most treasured gifts. By facing these aspects of ourselves, we become free to experience our glorious totality: the good and the bad, the dark and the light."*
>
> — DEBBIE FORD

MIRROR WORK EXERCISE FOR EMBRACING THE SHADOW

Objective

To use Mirror work as a tool for self-acceptance and integration of the Shadow, contributing to the process of individuation.

Materials Needed

A full-length mirror (or one that shows at least the upper half of your body)
A quiet, private space
A notebook and pen for reflections

Step 1.

Prepare Your Space

Choose a time and place where you won't be disturbed. Ensure the lighting is comfortable, neither too harsh nor too dim.

Step 2.

Relax and Center Yourself

Before starting, spend a few minutes in a calming practice, such as deep breathing, meditation, or gentle stretching. This helps to create a receptive state of mind.

Step 3.

Initial Gaze

Stand or sit in front of the mirror. Look into your own eyes and observe your reflection without judgment. Notice any immediate thoughts or emotions that arise.

Step 4.

Dialogue with Your Reflection

Begin to talk to your reflection as if it were a separate person. Address your positive traits and the aspects you consider your Shadow (e.g., insecurities, fears, perceived flaws). Acknowledge these aspects openly.

Step 5.

Affirmation and Acceptance

For each aspect you discuss, follow with an affirmation of acceptance. For example, "I acknowledge my anger, and I accept it as a part of me." This step is crucial for embracing all parts of yourself.

Step 6.

Embrace Your Shadow

Focus on the traits you usually avoid or dislike. Offer them compassion and understanding. Recognize that these aspects have played a role in your life and have contributed to your growth.

Step 7.

Reflect on Individuation

Consider how acknowledging and accepting these aspects can contribute to your journey towards wholeness. Recognize that individuation involves integrating these parts into your conscious self.

Step 8.

Journal Your Experience

After the session, write down your experiences, thoughts, and feelings in a notebook or on your device. Reflect on how your perception of yourself changes as you acknowledge and accept all parts of yourself.

Step 9.

Regular Practice

Repeat this exercise regularly. Over time, you may notice a shift in how you perceive and accept yourself, moving closer to individuation.

Step 10.

Insights

This exercise is about non-judgmental self-observation and acceptance. It's normal to experience discomfort or resistance, especially when confronting aspects of your Shadow.

Mirror work can be emotionally intense. If you find it overwhelming, take a break and consider seeking support from a therapist or a trusted confidant.

Try to do this exercise regularly as you begin your Shadow Work in earnest. As you progress, you may notice a reduced internal conflict and an increased sense of inner harmony. This indicates the integration of your Shadow and movement towards individuation.

It's also important to remember that individuation is a lifelong journey. Each step towards acceptance brings you closer to understanding and embracing your true, holistic self.

Shadow Work Chronicle – Ava's Story

"I came to Shadow Work after my Grandmother died. She was a Roma, and she didn't mind the term "gypsy". She read tea leaves and coffee cups, and people travelled from far and wide for her readings. As a kid, I thought it was all nonsense. But after she died, she kept coming to me in dreams – sometimes giving me warnings, other times just bathing me in love. At first, I wanted to ignore the messages, but the dreams became more intense and frequent, and I felt like someone was watching me. It was unnerving, so I went to a friend of my Gran's who also had the "sight", and she told me I was running away from my roots, heritage and true self. She encouraged me to investigate my own "sight", and to my amazement, I found I could instinctively read tea leaves like my Gran. I have gone deeply into the Shadow world, and I know its pitfalls and peaks. I wouldn't go back to my ignorance of that side of myself for a million bucks".

SHADOW SENTENCE COMPLETION

Now that you know some places to look for the external manifestations of the Shadow, the following exercise is designed to help you pinpoint where the tricky devil is hiding in the recesses of your personality.

This technique is based on Nathaniel Branden's sentence completion work, which is a tool for self-discovery and psychological change. The exercise promotes self-awareness, a key component in various psychological therapies, including Cognitive Behavioral Therapy (CBT).

Brandon's book The Six Pillars of Self-Esteem outlines these key principles as integral to becoming a whole person and living in a balanced and responsible way.

- **Living Consciously:** The practice of being aware of what you're doing while you're doing it—mindfulness.
- **Self-Acceptance:** Means owning truths regarding your thoughts, emotions, and behaviors. It also means being kind towards yourself with respect, self-compassion, and self-care.
- **Self-Responsibility:** Taking ownership of your actions and capacity for agency over your behaviours.
- **Self-Assertiveness:** Treating your needs and interests respectfully and expressing them in appropriate, non-harmful ways.
- **Living purposefully:** Formulating goals and implementing action plans to achieve them.
- **Personal Integrity:** Maintaining alignment between your convictions and behaviors.

Objective

To uncover subconscious thoughts and feelings related to your Shadow by completing open-ended sentences.

Step 1.

Sentence Starters: Write down a list of sentence starters related to feelings and behaviors you struggle with or find undesirable. For example, "I feel angry when...", "I wish I could stop...", or "I am afraid to admit that..."

Step 2.

Completion Exercise: Complete each sentence quickly, without overthinking. Write the first thing that comes to mind, even if it doesn't make sense or feels uncomfortable.

Step 3.

Reflective Review: After you've completed several sentences, go back and read them. Reflect on the themes and emotions that emerge.

Step 4.

Insight Integration: Choose one insight to explore further. How can this awareness help you to address the Shadow aspect in your life?

Step 5.

Benefit: Sentence completion can help bypass the conscious mind's filters, allowing deeper truths to surface. This can lead to breakthroughs in self-understanding and personal growth.

TOOLS FOR THE ROAD

Vulnerability

Vulnerability is the beating heart of authenticity. To venture into the Shadow is to engage in the sacred art of self-confrontation, where you must gather the courage to face the concealed fragments of your psyche.

Why is vulnerability critical for Shadow Work? Because it is the very essence that allows for transformation and healing. Vulnerability is the gentle yet powerful force that dismantles the walls around our innermost selves, permitting us to access and understand the hidden corners of our character. It is the key that unlocks the chains of our past, liberating us from the narratives that no longer serve our highest good.

When we allow ourselves to be vulnerable, we open up to the possibility of introspection and honesty that Shadow Work demands. It's a declaration of our willingness to acknowledge our darkness, learn from it, and integrate it into our whole being. Vulnerability is also the soil in which compassion blossoms, a nurturing environment where every aspect of our nature can be accepted and loved.

Perhaps the most crucial and least understood part of vulnerability in Shadow Work is that it paves the way for empathy. As we come to terms with our Shadows, we inherently grow more tolerant and understanding of others. Shadow work cultivates a deeper connection to the human experience–one that recognizes and embraces the full spectrum of human emotions and experience.

Setting Intentions for the Path Ahead

A fundamental step on the path of Shadow Work is setting intentions. When we delve into the labyrinth of our subconscious, we're venturing into a realm as vast and complex as it is enigmatic. Without a clear intention, we may wander aimlessly through our psyche's intricate corridors, becoming lost or overwhelmed by what we uncover.

An intention acts as a compass, pointing us toward our true north of self-discovery. It's a statement of purpose, a declaration to the universe and our subconscious that we are ready to face whatever lies in our Shadow with courage, honesty, and an open heart. Whether it's to heal old wounds, understand the origins of our fears, reconcile with parts of ourselves we've long rejected, or cultivate a more authentic, wild, and free life, our intentions keep us aligned with our goals.

In Shadow Work, setting intentions is an exercise in conscious commitment. It acknowledges that the process is significant and deserves our full presence. With clear intentions, we assert to ourselves that we're not undertaking this work lightly but with a solemn dedication to growth and self-love. This conscious commitment helps summon the psychological and spiritual energies needed to integrate our Shadows.

Intentions can also serve as a safeguard against the often-tumultuous emotions and revelations that Shadow Work can bring. They remind us why we started on this path when the journey becomes difficult. In moments of doubt or discomfort, our intentions can be an anchor that keeps us steady, a reminder of the big picture and healing that lies beyond the immediate pain.

Our intentions ensure that our efforts towards wholeness are constructive and guide us towards greater self-understanding and evolution.

Keep Your Wits About You with Clear Intentions

Your Shadow can be as slippery as a snake and as cunning as a rat. Setting clear and concise intentions and maintaining your awareness from moment to moment will help you flush out your inner darkness.

Here's how to do it.

Step 1.

Identify Your Goals: Ask yourself what you wish to achieve through Shadow Work. Do you want to heal a particular wound, change a behavior pattern, or understand certain emotional reactions? Be as specific as possible.

Step 2.

Formulate Clear Intentions: Turn your goals into clear and positive intentions. Phrase them in the present tense, as though they are already happening. For example, "I intend to embrace and understand my anger" instead of "I don't want to be angry."

Step 3.

Engage Your Emotions: As you set your intentions, try to connect with the feeling of what it will be like to achieve them. Emotions are powerful drivers that can solidify your commitment to your Shadow Work practice.

Step 4.

Affirm Your Intentions: You can speak your intentions out loud and record them, write them down, or meditate on them. Affirming them in a way that feels powerful to you helps to embed them in your subconscious.

Step 5.

Let Go of Attachment: Release any attachment to outcomes. Trust that the process will guide you where you need to go, even if it's not where you expected.

Step 6.

Return to Your Intentions: Regularly remind yourself of your intentions. This can be through daily affirmations, revisiting your journal, or setting aside time for reflection.

Your intentions are not set in stone. They will evolve as you progress in your Shadow Work. Revisit and revise them as needed to align with your growing self-awareness and changing circumstances.

HELP FOR THE TOUGH STUFF

Processing the difficult emotions that arise during Shadow Work takes some skill. There are a few things to set in place as you begin the sometimes challenging and often emotional part of excavating your secret self. For a start, set boundaries. You need to set some limits on the time you spend delving into the darkness and exercise some caution as you progress. It can be intoxicating exploring the unnavigated parts of your psyche, but you also need to stay grounded. Make sure you exercise, eat a nutritious diet, get adequate hydration and take time out to spend in nature and ground yourself–take your shoes and socks off and allow your feet the pleasure of standing on solid ground. This simple grounding exercise is profoundly important. Shadow Work can be like slipping into quicksand, so you need to stay rooted to the earth and self-aware. In the same vein, practice some pranayama or deep breathing (steps below) to keep you in your body and nourish your heart.

On the topic of boundaries, you may find you need to set some boundaries with friends and family members, too. When you start doing this work, relationships often change. There are strategies in this book about how to manage some difficult scenarios, but you may also find some friends (and sadly, sometimes family members too) whose past and present behaviours no longer accord with your objectives for yourself and your growth. Negotiating new rules of engagement with people you've known for a long time can be challenging.

In all this, I recommend making changes gradually and with loads of self-love and compassion. Also, allow a feeling of empathy for the people you may be leaving behind to bubble up. People will often be confused about your transformation, and if you don't want to be overt about the deep work you're doing, it can be tricky to explain how and why you've changed. You'll need to find a balance between being kind and compassionate and asserting your new rules.

In my own life, I've found yoga, EFT tapping, meditation, creative visualisation, drawing and deep breathing (obviously not all at once) work wonders when I'm feeling overwhelmed by the challenges of Shadow Work. At the very least, I urge you to employ this breathing exercise on a daily basis to help you release any negative emotions and ground yourself in the moment.

HEART-CENTERED PRANAYAMA BREATHING ROUTINE FOR PRESENT MOMENT AWARENESS

Step 1.

Prepare

In a quiet space, sit comfortably with your spine erect or lie flat. Relax your body with a few natural breaths and place one hand over your heart to connect with your heart center.

Step 2.

Inhale and Hold

Slowly inhale through your nose to a count of four, feeling your heart rise beneath your hand. Hold this breath for a count of four, tuning into your heartbeat.

Step 3.

Exhale and Pause

Gently exhale to a count of six, envisioning any stress or tension being released. Pause for two counts before your next breath, enjoying the stillness.

Step 4.

Visualize and Set an Intention

With each cycle, visualize a warm light in your heart center growing brighter and set an intention of love or healing to infuse your practice.

Step 5.

Conclude with Gratitude

After several minutes, let your breathing return to normal and your hand rest. Reflect on the feelings of warmth and expansion, ending with a silent thank you for the self-care you've practiced.

EMOTIONAL RESCUE

In the transformative but intense self-exploration that is Shadow Work, being able to recognize and manage emotional overwhelm is crucial. Feelings of overwhelm may surface as a surge of unexpected emotions, physical symptoms like anxiety or fatigue, or a feeling of mental paralysis. It often happens when the mind and body react to the dredging up of suppressed memories and feelings that Shadow Work brings to the surface.

Managing overwhelm begins with acknowledging it. During these times, it's beneficial to reach out for support from trusted friends, a support group, or a professional therapist who can provide a safe space for you to express and work through these intense feelings.

Emotional first aid, such as heart-centred breathing, should be your immediate go-to when you feel a sudden wave of emotional distress. Self-soothing practices like holding a warm cup of tea, wrapping up in a soft blanket, or listening to calming music can also help.

Understanding when to seek help is paramount. If you find that the overwhelm is persistent, impacting your daily functioning, or leading to harmful thoughts, it is time to seek professional help. A mental health professional skilled in trauma work can offer strategies tailored to your needs and can guide you safely through the more challenging aspects of Shadow Work.

Navigating the waters of emotional overwhelm with these strategies in your toolkit ensures that your journey through Shadow Work remains a healing and enriching process—guiding you towards the wholeness that lies within.

Acknowledging Wins

It's true that Shadow Work takes time, and progress can often feel painstakingly slow. It's crucial to normalize and accept your own pace because such deep work requires time, patience, and a gentle approach. One thing is sure: peeling back the layers of the psyche cannot be rushed, and resolving past wounds cannot be forced. Steady, incremental progress is not only safer but also a sign of sustainable growth.

To cultivate patience, consider mindfulness practices that anchor you in the present moment, such as meditation or conscious breathing (above). These can help alleviate the pressure of reaching the end goal quickly and instead shift the focus to the ongoing process of growth. Also, setting aside regular times for reflection can allow you to monitor your progress without judgment, keeping the bigger picture in perspective.

Celebrating small wins is another essential strategy. It could be as simple as acknowledging the courage it took to face a particular memory or emotion. These milestones, no matter how small, are the building blocks of your journey and deserve recognition. Each one is a step toward greater self-awareness and should be celebrated.

The value of persistence in Shadow Work cannot be overstated. It's a path marked by periods of intensity and tranquillity, each offering invaluable lessons. Repeated return to this inner work, even when progress seems elusive and painful, forges resilience and facilitates true transformation. Staying the course is not about the speed of travel but the depth of the journey.

Managing Objections and Cultivating the Right Mindset

Shadow Work has its naysayers. Many in the therapeutic world question its benefits and relevance. As I said earlier, Jungian therapy has been eschewed in recent years in favour of faster therapeutic techniques. Don't be too surprised if you encounter scepticism and feel compelled to counter some misconceptions.

Those sceptical about the benefits might question the practicality of exploring one's darker nature. Others fear the discomfort that comes from facing suppressed memories or disowned parts of the self. It's not uncommon to worry about what might be found or whether it's safe to confront such depths.

Compassionate responses to these objections can be best managed by acknowledging the concerns while also asserting your personal right to choose your own path to healing. You may start by explaining that this is not about dwelling in darkness but about bringing light to the unexplored aspects of your being. Your experience is your best guide and model–no one can argue with your valid personal experience.

One powerful myth that circulated around therapeutic communities is the notion that Shadow Work is an endless journey into sorrow. It's simply not true–it's a profoundly enlivening, self-loving exploration that provides a route to liberation and wholeness, a process that, though it may involve difficult emotions and painful investigations, leads to a much greater sense of peace and wholeness. Research into therapeutic practices that encompass aspects of Shadow Work, such as Jungian therapy and cognitive-behavioral therapy, underscores the transformative effects of integrating all parts of the self–including those once hidden from view.

ONE FOR THE ROAD

If I can impart any advice, it would be to cultivate an open mind and heart. Consider the power of self-knowledge as a key not just to personal liberation but also to deeper connections with everyone in your life. Shadow Work is not simply a practice but an invitation to experience the full spectrum of who you are, so you emerge not only intact but vitally renewed. It's a personal expedition, and only by walking the path can you truly understand the richness and power it has to offer.

> *"Traveler, there is no path.*
> *The path is made by walking.*
> *Traveller, the path is your tracks*
> *And nothing more.*
> *Traveller, there is no path*
> *The path is made by walking.*
> *By walking you make a path*
> *And turning, you look back*
> *At a way you will never tread again*
> *Traveller, there is no road*
> *Only wakes in the sea."*
>
> — ANTONIO MACHADO

Never forget, you are your own wise guide. You are your own Oracle.

CHAPTER THREE

DIALOGUING WITH THE SHADOW

OK, so your loved ones and friends might think you're a little crazy when they hear you have a two-way conversation with yourself in the shower, but you'll have to give up caring about what anyone else thinks while you do this work.

Dialoguing with the Shadow unlocks a rich store (or sometimes a Pandora's box) of untapped potential. This intimate conversation is not just courageous but liberating. As you get to know the voice of your innermost self, you'll discover that your Shadow is not an enemy stalking your psyche but a powerful ally waiting for recognition.

Embracing your Shadow illuminates the path to self-mastery, revealing the full spectrum of your strengths hidden beneath layers of fear and societal expectations. By integrating these forsaken fragments, you'll create a life of authenticity and freedom. Imagine if every decision was power-packed with self-awareness, where you navigate the world with the quiet confidence of someone who truly knows themselves. That's more than great, it's incredible!

You'll be amazed by the messages available to you when you embrace the Shadow. Intuition, gut feelings, nagging voices, whispers and calls from beyond our material world are all Oracles. If you wish to be the bearer, herald and interpreter of these subtle calls, you'll need to tune your hearing into their enigmatic messages.

As you venture through this chapter, let each carefully crafted question guide you deeper into your psyche, transforming shadows of doubt into bright rays of insight. Your life will change in unimaginable ways. This is not just self-improvement; it's self-revolution. Welcome to the conversation of a lifetime.

This chapter is all about communication–an inner conversation with those parts of yourself you've just begun to acknowledge. This is where the transformation and deep healing *really* begin. *Your initiation into the psychic realms of becoming an Oracle literally starts when you can tune into the song of your own subtle voice.*

Here, you'll explore your Shadow's needs and desires through Socratic questioning, a method that encourages deep thinking and self-inquiry; Reflective Writing, which helps you get into the head-space of your Shadow; Affirmation Work and NLP, or Neuro-Linguistic Programming, which provides a direct and powerful way to step into your Shadow's shoes. Finally, and most importantly, you'll learn some powerful techniques for *honing your intuition–your direct channel to becoming the Oracle you were always meant to be.*

The writing exercises in this chapter are in two parts. First, grab a notebook and answer the Socratic Questions as honestly as you possibly can. They'll give you loads of insights to complete the second part of the exercise, the Shadow Work Journaling.

Dialoguing with your Shadow is an empowering process. It allows you to understand your deeper motivations, fears, and desires. This understanding is crucial in making conscious choices that are aligned with your true self and your values. Embrace this chapter as an opportunity to deepen your self-knowledge and foster an integrated and harmonious inner world.

Are you ready to become both the messenger and the message? Discovering that awesome power begins now!

> *"Light and shadow are opposite sides of the same coin. We can illuminate our paths or darken our way. It is a matter of choice."*
>
> — MAYA ANGELOU

30 SOCRATIC QUESTIONS TO FACILITATE CONVERSATION WITH YOUR SHADOW

- What emotions do I feel when I think about my Shadow?
- When do I notice my Shadow influencing my actions the most?
- What specific situations seem to trigger a response from my Shadow?
- What are the common themes in the things that trigger my Shadow?
- What might my Shadow be trying to communicate through these triggers?
- How do these Shadow-triggered reactions serve me, or how have they served me in the past?
- In what ways have I allowed my Shadow to make decisions for me?
- What are the positive and negative aspects of these Shadow-influenced decisions?
- How does my Shadow reflect my unmet needs or desires?
- What would happen if I fully embraced the aspects of my Shadow?
- How does my Shadow contribute to my sense of self and identity?
- What fears do I have about confronting my Shadow?
- How can my Shadow teach me about parts of myself I am not fully conscious of?
- What lessons have I learned from the times my Shadow has come to the surface?
- How might my life change if I integrate my Shadow aspects more fully?

- What would I say to my Shadow if it were a person sitting in front of me?
- How does my Shadow react to the different roles I play in my life?
- Are there aspects of my Shadow that I admire or find strength in?
- How does my Shadow influence my relationships with others?
- What does my Shadow need from me to feel acknowledged and understood?
- How has my Shadow affected my personal growth and development?
- What would it look like to have a healthy relationship with my Shadow?
- In what ways have I been unfair or unjust to my Shadow?
- How can I show compassion to the parts of myself that I consider to be my Shadow?
- What is the origin of the parts of me that I identify as my Shadow?
- How does my cultural background and upbringing influence my perception of my Shadow?
- What does my resistance to certain Shadow aspects say about my values and beliefs?
- How can I use my Shadow to guide me toward what I truly want in life?
- How does acknowledging my Shadow affect the authenticity of my actions?
- What steps can I take to foster a continuous and open dialogue with my Shadow?

The purpose of these questions is to encourage you to reflect on the less-conscious parts of your psyche to facilitate a process of understanding and integration. If you'd like to do it as a 30-day program, you could take one question each day and really dive into it. It's up to you how you approach this exercise.

Remember, the Shadow is not an adversary but a teacher, guide and compass that will ultimately lead you to a more authentic, self-accepting, self-loving and fulfilling life.

REFLECTIVE WRITING OR SHADOW JOURNALING

Objective

Using the insights gained by answering the Socratic Questions take some time to develop even greater insights into your Shadow-self by using journaling and reflective writing.

Step 1.

Consistent Practice: Set aside time each day for 30 days to write in your journal. Focus on reflecting on events or interactions that triggered a strong emotional response.

Step 2.

Detail Exploration: Write about the details of these events and explore why they might have triggered such a response.

Step 3.

Emotion Dissection: Examine the underlying emotions and thoughts that these triggers brought up. What might they be saying about your Shadow?

Step 4.

Behavioral Patterns: Look for patterns in your behavior that may indicate a Shadow aspect influencing your actions.

Step 5.

Integration Intent: Write about how you might integrate and accept these Shadow aspects to diminish their negative impact on your life.

Step 6.

Benefit: Journaling can provide a safe space to explore difficult emotions and thoughts, leading to greater self-awareness and personal growth.

Nixing The Negatives

When we look in the mirror and don't like what we see, embracing our wholeness can be challenging. Most people want to shun an aspect of themselves, believing it's not fit for public consumption. If any of these statements sound familiar, then I'm talking to you!

- I'm hateful.
- I'm too fat.
- I'm too loud.
- No one likes me.
- I'm disgusting.
- I'm unlovable.
- I'm worthless.
- I'm incompetent.
- I'm unattractive.
- I'm weak.
- I'm a failure.
- I'm too awkward.
- I'm a disappointment.
- I'm useless.
- I'm not smart enough.

- I'm unwanted.
- I'm insignificant.
- I'm invisible.
- I'm a burden.
- I'm not enough.
- I'm hopeless.
- I'm damaged.
- I'm disliked.
- I'm a loser.
- I'm too emotional.
- I'm not worthy.

If any or many of these statements resonated with you, then you'll have a good idea of the power the Shadow has over you and its effects on your self-esteem.

One of the fastest and most effective ways to combat the negativity the Shadow can exert over your self-confidence is to work with affirmations.

You can start by simply counteracting the statements above. For example, when you hear your inner voice whisper, "I'm a failure", you can counter with, "I'm a success", but if you want to work more deeply, these Shadow-Work-Specific affirmations will help you rewrite negative-self-talk and negative self-beliefs and can even help heal past traumas.

Scientifically, affirmations have been shown to stimulate the areas in our brain that make us more likely to affect positive changes regarding our health. A study published in the journal "Social Cognitive and Affective Neuroscience" found that self-affirmation activates the ventromedial prefrontal cortex, a region associated with positive valuation and self-related information processing.

This activation suggests a neurophysiological basis for how affirmations can improve our perception of self-worth and our ability to face challenges.

By incorporating Shadow-Work-Specific affirmations into your daily routine, you're taking a step towards healing and embracing all parts of yourself, including those you may have once viewed negatively.

> *"Our deepest fear is not that we are inadequate. Our deepest fear is that we are powerful beyond measure. It is our light, not our darkness that most frightens us. We ask ourselves, 'Who am I to be brilliant, gorgeous, talented, fabulous?'"*
>
> — MARIANNE WILLIAMSON

30 SHADOW-WORK-SPECIFIC AFFIRMATIONS

- I embrace all aspects of myself with compassion and understanding.
- My Shadow is a part of me, and I accept it with love.
- Even as I work through my shadows, I am worthy of love and respect.
- I release the hold that past traumas have on my present self.
- My mistakes and flaws are stepping stones to growth and self-improvement.
- I am learning to accept and integrate my hidden aspects.
- I am more than my negative thoughts and beliefs.
- Each day, I grow stronger and more in tune with my true self.

- I choose to respond to my Shadow with curiosity, not fear.
- My Shadow traits are not my enemy; they are guides to deeper understanding.
- I am deserving of forgiveness from others and myself.
- My challenges and struggles are opportunities for transformation.
- I am capable of changing patterns that no longer serve me.
- I honor my feelings, even those that are uncomfortable.
- My journey of self-discovery leads to a place of peace and acceptance.
- I am patient with myself as I explore the depths of my being.
- I acknowledge my fears and face them with courage.
- I am a work in progress, and that is perfectly okay.
- My inner world is rich and complex, and I embrace its entirety.
- Every part of me deserves to be heard and understood.
- I am learning to love the person I am becoming.
- I let go of self-judgment and embrace self-awareness.
- My Shadow shows me where healing is needed.
- I control how I perceive and react to my inner world.
- I replace self-criticism with self-compassion.
- I am on a journey towards wholeness and inner peace.
- I welcome all parts of myself into the light of consciousness.
- I am strong enough to face the hidden aspects of my psyche.
- I trust in my ability to integrate my Shadow for greater harmony.
- My journey through Shadow Work leads me to authentic self-expression.

These positive statements help ***reframe your inner critic's narrative***, enabling you to shift from a mindset of self-judgment to one of self-compassion and acceptance. Affirmations can help heal past traumas by altering negative thought patterns and promoting positive changes in the brain.

NLP FOR INSIGHT

Neuro-Linguistic Programming (NLP) is an approach to communication, personal development, and psychotherapy created by Richard Bandler and John Grinder in the 1970s. It's based on the idea that there's a connection between neurological processes ("neuro"), language ("linguistic"), and behavioral patterns learned through experience ("programming"). NLP suggests that by adjusting how we perceive the world, we can alter our thoughts, feelings, and behaviors.

Practitioners use various techniques, including visualization, reframing, and language patterns, to help clients reshape their mental landscape. The goal of NLP is to help people understand their own minds, how they operate, and how they can direct their thoughts and emotions in ways more aligned with their values, goals and dreams. Although it's popular amongst coaches and counsellors, and I've found it very useful myself, the empirical scientific support for NLP is limited, so before you start any psychological process, such as NLP, check in with your doctor or psychotherapist.

NLP Exercise: Parts Integration Technique

Objective

To help resolve internal disharmony and create a bridge between the conflicting parts of the psyche.

Step 1.

Identify Conflicting Parts

Begin by identifying two parts of your psyche that seem to conflict. For example, one part of you wants to be more outgoing, while another part holds back due to fear of rejection.

Step 2.

Spatial Anchoring

Assign each part a physical space or 'anchor'. Stand in one spot to represent the first part of your psyche and another spot for the second part. These should be a few feet apart. You can also use chairs to represent the different parts of your psyche.

Step 3.

Part Exploration

In the space of the first part, embody it fully. Speak as that part, expressing its desires, fears, and purpose. Ask, "What is your positive intention?" NLP posits that every behavior has a positive intention at its core. Then, step into the space of the second part and do the same. You'll be moving around the room–don't worry if it seems weird. Just carry on with the exercise.

Step 4.

Discover Common Intentions

Look for a higher-level common intention between the two parts. Even conflicting parts often have overlapping positive intentions, such as protection, success, or well-being.

Step 5.

Visualize Integration

Imagine a dialogue between the two parts, where each acknowledges the other's positive intentions. Visualize a negotiation where they work together to serve the higher common intention.

Step 6.

Create a New Part

Imagine a third space where the two parts can merge, taking the strengths and intentions from each. Step into this space and feel the integration as a new, unified part of your psyche.

Step 7.

Future Pacing

Imagine moving forward in time with this newly integrated part. Visualize how it changes your behavior and feelings in situations where you previously experienced conflict.

Step 8.

Anchor the New State

Create a physical or mental anchor (like touching your fingers or clapping your hands together) that you can use to quickly access this state of integration in the future.

Step 9.

Test and Validate

Think about a situation that would have caused internal conflict before. Use your anchor and notice if you feel more aligned and harmonious.

Step 10.

Reflection and Journaling

After completing the exercise, reflect on the experience and journal any insights or shifts in perspective.

Step 11.

Outcome

By the end of this exercise, the previously conflicting parts should feel more aligned, reducing internal conflict and promoting a sense of internal harmony. This technique helps ensure that different aspects of the psyche work together for a common, **positive** outcome.

Note

This exercise is based on the NLP concept that the mind comprises semi-independent parts that can be communicated with and integrated. It utilizes a technique called "spatial anchoring" to physically represent psychological concepts–a common NLP strategy to make abstract concepts more tangible and easier to work with.

DEVELOPING YOUR SIXTH SENSE TO BECOME THE ORACLE

What if I told you that the power tool for lifelong protection and guidance is none other than your intuition? High performers across business, sports and the arts will readily swear by their sixth sense. It's an entirely human superpower that absolutely everyone has. It allows us to make decisions in a split-second without over-thinking or missing moments. And more than that, it's a highway between your more ethereal subconscious self and your conscious mind.

There's even a 2016 scientific study to prove that intuition is real–and powerful. Researchers from the School of Psychology at the University of New South Wales found that the brain can simultaneously process all sorts of information from different directions to make behavioral decisions. "Although the exact neural architecture responsible for the effects we observed [the processing of different sources of information], our data show that under the right circumstances, something that resembles the general description of intuition does indeed exist, can be precisely and reliably measured and manipulated using our novel paradigm, and can be modelled using existing decision models", the authors report.

Luckily, you don't have to be a high-flier, an uber-athlete, a shaman, a healer or a mystic to have the confidence to go with your gut. The following tools will help you tune in, listen to, and act in a way that aligns with your intuition, helping you make powerful, self-loving decisions.

Practice for Progress

Actively tuning into your intuition and having a supportive daily practice that hones it, such as automatic journaling, visualisation, meditation, and creative expression will sharpen this vital sense.

To be clear, there isn't much scientific evidence currently available to verify the power of these practices in developing your gut instincts. However, they will contribute to your sense of well-being and agency, whether science can prove them or not.

Step 1.

Prioritize Your Intuition

We are constantly bombarded by data. When you add into the mix the fact that our culture prizes rationality and science over subtle senses like intuition, it's not surprising that many of us find it challenging to listen to our intuition and let it flow.

Yet, free flow, from the emotional and psychic centres of the self to the conscious mind, is precisely what we need to accomplish to "hear" the messages. If you're not used to trusting your intuition in decision-making, the key is to allow time for answers to come to you without overanalysing.

Make time each day, or even several times a day if you have an important decision, to tune into your intuition. Allow it to bubble up to the surface and try not to suppress it with judgements or overlay it with societal expectations. Letting it speak to you, hearing its whispers and shouts, is a shortcut to personal power and agency.

Step 2.

Figure Out How the Oracle 'Speaks' to You

People experience intuition differently. For some, it may present as an image; for others, it may be a physical sensation (the classic 'gut feeling'); yet others may identify a more emotional response, such as a rush of feelings and an "Ah-ha" moment. The idea is to slow down and try to sense how or where you experience your intuitions. Does it manifest in your mind, your heart or your whole body? Is it a comfortable, comforting sensation, or raw, unbridled, and scary? Make a note of how your intuitive feelings move and guide you to action. You'll start to get clear about whether it's your intuition you're tuning into or a voice from somewhere else in yourself, such as the voice of your parents, authority figures or a repressed inner child? Helpful hint: The voice of your intuition is usually clear, unequivocal, courageous and assertive.

Step 3.

Maintain Your Oracle Journal

Write down your hunches in a journal and notice how the voice speaks to you. It is particularly beneficial to capture them before the analytic process takes over. Try not to be tempted to analyse or overthink your intuitions. They're straight from your unconscious, and whilst the mind wants to filter them (to stay safe and comfortable and out of harm's way), sometimes your intuition wants the exact opposite. Let the information flow from the depths of your psyche without filtering or fiddling with them.

One helpful trick is to keep your journal with you during the day. Write down your gut feelings about a situation or decision in real time. Later, you can check to assess how accurate or helpful they were.

Writing down words, phrases, images, and ideas as they come to you when considering a problem may also provide different insights. Drawing without judging how good your drawings are or whether they're perfect representations is a great way to slow down the process and tap into more intuitive modes of thinking.

Step 4.

Use Mindfulness and Meditation Techniques to Tap into The Oracle

Mindfulness and meditation encourage us to notice feelings and thoughts without attaching to them. This can be very useful if you are trying to develop your intuition. Watching and accepting thoughts without judgment will allow you deeper access to intuitive information.

The body scan mindfulness technique, where you breathe into a different part of your body—from the toes to the crown—can help you become aware of sensations in your body that might relate to intuitive processing. A body scan can be done whenever you have an important decision to make, or if you want to build it like a muscle and improve its efficiency, simply practice daily to improve your intuition.

Here's how to do it.

Body scanning meditation is a popular mindfulness practice that involves systematically scanning different parts of the body, bringing attention and awareness to each area.

- **Preparation:** Find a comfortable and quiet space to sit or lie down without distractions. Close your eyes if that feels comfortable, but it's not necessary.
- **Grounding:** Begin by taking a few deep breaths, allowing yourself to arrive fully in the present moment. Feel the weight of your body on the chair or the floor and notice any sensations or sounds around you.
- **Starting Point:** Start the scan at one end of your body, either at the top of your head or the tips of your toes. Choose whichever feels more natural to you.
- **Systematic Attention:** Slowly and methodically move your attention through each part of your body, one by one. You can start with your toes or the top of your head and move towards the opposite end or vice versa. Commonly, the sequence might be feet, lower legs, knees,

thighs, pelvis, abdomen, chest, back, shoulders, arms, hands, neck, face, and head.

- **Notice Sensations:** As you focus on each part, pay attention to any sensations you may be experiencing without judgment. This could include warmth, coldness, tingling, tension, or relaxation. Observe whatever arises without trying to change it.
- **Release Tension:** If you notice any tension or discomfort, imagine breathing into those areas with each inhale and releasing tension with each exhale. You can also intentionally relax each muscle group as you scan through it.
- **Non-Judgmental Awareness:** Throughout the practice, maintain an attitude of curiosity and non-judgment. If your mind wanders, gently bring your attention back to the sensations in your body without criticizing yourself.
- **Completion:** Once you've scanned your entire body, take a few moments to rest in awareness, noticing the overall sensation of your body. Slowly bring your attention back to your surroundings, gently wiggle your fingers and toes, and when you're ready, open your eyes.

Step 5.

Ten Questions to Tap into The Oracle's Gifts

These questions are specifically designed to fast-track your journey from a vague hunch in the pit of your stomach or a fluttering of butterflies in your heart to your mind. Think of it as a train that carries important messages from your unconscious self directly to your conscious mind.

- "Does it feel like the right thing to do?"
- "Does it seem like the right answer?"
- "How do I feel when I think about x situation?"
- "What was my gut reaction?"
- "Do I have a hunch about that?"
- "Where in my body do I notice a reaction?"
- "If I already knew the answer, what would it be?"
- "Is this sense coming from my higher self or another voice such as my parents, teachers or institutions?"
- "Why am I uncomfortable?"
- "Is this decision for my benefit? Will I be spiritually, emotionally, physically, financially, creatively or otherwise better off?"

This is powerful juju. Practice listening to the messages, and you will become the Oracle–and from there, the sky's the limit. What you'll have at your disposal is the most potent psychic weapon imaginable–the lightsabre of your higher self. And just as a lightsabre can cut through things, your intuition has the power to cut through the crap and get to the truth of a situation.

Whether you're deciding to take a job, end a relationship, start a new partnership, travel overseas, or even do something mundane, such as which bus to catch when you're lost, your intuition acts as a guiding light whose sole aim is to take you on the path of your higher self. Listen to it, trust it, and allow it to act as a signpost, and you'll discover untold treasures.

Shadow Chronicle – Lily's Story

Trigger Warning. This story contains sexual abuse. If you need help, please seek professional medical and psychological advice.

"I had good reason to hide my rage; it was the only way I could survive my childhood abuse. When I was 11 years old, my uncle sexually abused me at a cousin's birthday party. I slipped off to the toilet at the back of the house, away from the party. As I came out of the bathroom, wiping my hands on my party dress, my uncle came forward with a towel. He was all smiles and smoothness. He said he wanted to show me something in my cousin's bedroom. Innocently, I followed him, and for a second thought, it was weird that he closed the door behind me. He got me onto the bed, and that's where it happened – the abuse, I mean. I didn't tell anyone about it. I pretended it didn't happen. I convinced myself that I had made it up and I was a horrible person for the feelings I was feeling. All the stress of that suppression made me sick, and I had chronic pain in my joints for years. It wasn't until I was in my mid-20s and went to therapy that I was able to unpack the incident and all the trauma that went with it and allow the justifiable rage, sadness and pain to come to the surface. Shadow Work isn't something you do once, it's an everyday thing, but I know if I hadn't unpacked all that suffering, I would have gone mad... or worse. Today, I can accept the unacceptable and also accept myself".

THE POWER OF INTEGRATION – SIGHTS AND SOUNDS FROM BEYOND THE EGO

When the Shadow is integrated and lives in harmony with the ego, you stop denying parts of yourself and begin to accept all aspects of your being. This acceptance reduces internal conflict and leads to psychological wholeness.

Integrating the Shadow gives you access to more psychological and psychic power. This power is not about control over others but about a deeper connection with your own capabilities and potential. What results is individuation, or the integration of the unconscious with the conscious, the dark and the light—leading to self-actualization.

And from that place of inner harmony, we are much more open to the wisdom that comes from the Oracle inside ourselves. This guidance can come through dreams, intuitions, and insights that seem to arise spontaneously. Jung believed that the subconscious mind communicates through symbols and archetypes, which can provide profound wisdom when understood and interpreted correctly (and you'll explore them in depth in the next chapter).

The end goal of Shadow Work is not just to integrate the light and dark aspects of yourself, it's more, so much more. The end goal here is to be able to tune into the psychic realms, usually reserved for shamans, mystics, healers and diviners of sacred messages and transform to become your own Oracle.

Are you ready to be initiated?

CHAPTER FOUR

ARCHETYPES FOR ILLUMINATION

Glimpsing your Shadow is like standing at the threshold of a hidden garden— you're aware of its existence but have yet to step inside and experience its intoxicating beauty. To truly flourish, you must step boldly and brazenly into the garden, inhale its exotic aromas, feel the cool grass at your feet and embrace its mysteries. This chapter is an invitation not just to observe but to engage fully with your Shadow, to hold it close, listen intently to its quiet mutterings and learn its untold stories.

The act of holding your Shadow close is an act of radical self-love. It's recognising that every aspect of your being—light and dark—is worthy of acceptance. This embrace is not a one-time affair; it's a lifelong romance with the deepest parts of your soul. In this sacred union, you'll find the true path to wholeness. When you welcome your Shadow with open arms, you unlock a reservoir of untapped strength and resilience.

Prepare to delve into practices that will guide you to acknowledge, negotiate with, and ultimately love all facets of your unique self. By integrating your Shadow, you illuminate the full spectrum of your personality, and it's here, in the synthesis of self, that you discover the profound wholeness that's been waiting all your life for you to be courageous and show up for yourself.

Carl Jung said, "Everyone carries a shadow", he maintained that the less it is embodied in the individual's conscious life, the blacker and denser it is. At all counts, it forms an unconscious snag, thwarting our most well-meant intentions. This book aims to help you live not only more freely, independently and authentically but also to access your power. Your genuine power lies in becoming who you were always meant to be–no roadblocks, no self-loathing and no self-sabotage. Now, being real, this is a lifelong path, not a quick fix; there are no magic bullets here. This is about doing The Work–Shadow Work. But my hope for you is that by dancing with your Shadow, you'll get in touch with your power and be able to release it to live your best life.

In this chapter, you're going to meet your archetypal self. It can come in the form of dream imagery and, according to Jung and philosophers such as Joseph Campbell, in subtle archetypes that we see repeated in art and literature, movies and divination tools like tarot and angelic symbols. These archetypes are common across cultures and religions, and you may find that you already know the characters that work through your psyche in enigmatic ways.

Integrating the archetypes into your practice is a shortcut to self-understanding. Even if you don't feel you naturally relate to one single archetype, you may find you resonate with a few traits. Between the 12 Jungian Archetypes and the images and symbols in your dreams, you will soon see that we are all subject to mysterious and even magical energies that permeate our souls at deep and unconscious levels.

We're on a heroic journey. The quest to unify ourselves is universal and sublimely human. You'll discover how the archetypes from dreams, myths and stories influence your path and bring both challenges and enlightenment.

STAGES OF EMBRACE

When Jung explored how the Shadow can be identified in the psyche, he outlined a four-stage process that involved ***Confession, Illumination, Education, and Transformation*** in the context of personal development and individuation.

Confession: Involves acknowledging and accepting the hidden, repressed, or denied parts of oneself. It's a process similar to the admission of sins in a religious context, but in psychological terms, it refers to becoming conscious of one's Shadow.

Illumination: Is the stage of gaining insight and enlightenment about oneself. It involves understanding the unconscious material brought to light through confession and integrating this understanding into one's consciousness.

Education: This is the phase in which the person learns how to live in harmony with their newly found insights and understanding. It involves adapting to the realities of life with a more integrated and holistic approach.

Transformation: The final stage of profound change in the personality is when the person has not only unearthed and understood the various aspects of their psyche but has also learned to live in a new, more authentic, unified and harmonious way, leading to a fundamental transformation of the self.

All these stages represent the way we engage with the Shadow. From our first tentative steps, as we *Confess* to ourselves and the world what our dark side is made of, to the *Illumination* stage, where we gain more profound enlightenment about ourselves, through to *Education*, where we really learn to live in harmony with who we are and begin the early stages of falling in deep love with ourselves, and finally, to *Transformation*, where we have fully and wholeheartedly accepted and embraced our true selves.

Where do you think you're at in the four stages of embracing your Shadow?

Look carefully at the four stages of engagement with the Shadow and do a journaling exercise where you write about the stage you're in right now. Review it in six months to assess your progress.

ARCHETYPES FOR INSIGHT

This process of evolving through the stages of getting to know who you really are rarely takes days or weeks. It usually takes months and sometimes years to work through these phases of insight.

To help people delve deeper into the often-abstract and enigmatic world of the Shadow, Jung also developed a system to understand personality using 12 archetypes: ***The Artist, The Innocent, The Sage, The Explorer, The Outlaw, The Magician, The Hero, The Lover, The Jester, The Everyman/Woman, The Caregiver and The Ruler.***

According to Jungian psychology, archetypes form the foundation for all human's common experiences. Jung believed people build their own experiences and interpretations on this foundation, influenced by their culture, personality, and life events. He posited that these archetypes give rise to various images, symbols, and behaviors.

Like symbols that appear in dreams, the 12 archetypes Jung described are common to most cultures, myths and stories from around the world and have appeared over and over since the beginning of time. Cave paintings depict the Hero and the Sage as they kill beasts and bring them back to the campsite to share with members of the tribe. Egyptian tomb paintings revealed virtually every one of the archetypes, and Greek and Roman myths are full of Jesters, Magicians, Rulers, Caregivers, Lovers and Artists.

Discovering which archetype you relate to most can give you more valuable insights into your psyche and Shadow.

There are similar free quizzes on the internet, but I've created this ***12 Archetypes Personality Quiz*** to give you awareness of which archetype may be playing out in your psyche. Treat this as a fun awareness and learning exercise, not a serious psychological evaluation.

QUIZ – WHO ARE YOU?

JUNG'S 12 PERSONALITY ARCHETYPES

Instructions

Choose the option you feel most deeply resonates with how you see yourself or act in most situations. There are no right or wrong answers.

Question 1: When I encounter a problem, I usually:

- A: Look for a creative or original solution.
- B: Try maintaining a positive outlook and looking for the good in the situation.
- C: Seek knowledge or wisdom to understand the problem better.
- D: Venture out to find new ways of solving it.
- E: Challenge the status quo or think outside the box.
- F: Use my intuition or come up with an innovative approach.
- G: Tackle it head-on with courage and determination.
- H: Engage with the problem passionately and with all my heart.
- I: Try to lighten the mood with humor or take it lightly.
- J: Deal with it in a practical, down-to-earth manner.
- K: Look out for others affected by the problem and help them first.

- L: Take charge and organize a plan to solve the problem efficiently.

Question 2: I feel most fulfilled when:

- A: I can express myself creatively and inspire others.
- B: I'm living in the moment and doing the right thing.
- C: I'm learning or teaching something valuable.
- D: I'm experiencing new things and exploring the world.
- E: I'm breaking the rules or challenging conventions.
- F: I'm transforming or changing something for the better.
- G: I'm overcoming obstacles and achieving my goals.
- H: I'm in a romantic relationship or deeply connected with someone.
- I: I'm making people laugh or enjoying myself.
- J: I'm being a good friend and a solid presence in someone's life.
- K: I care for others and make a difference in their lives.
- L: I'm leading a group or project to success.

Question 3: My friends would describe me as someone who is:

- A: Creative and artistic.
- B: Optimistic and trusting.
- C: Wise and insightful.
- D: Independent and adventurous.
- E: Rebellious and bold.
- F: Charismatic and dynamic.
- G: Brave and heroic.
- H: Affectionate and passionate.
- I: Fun-loving and humorous.
- J: Reliable and down-to-earth.

- K: Nurturing and supportive.
- L: Authoritative and influential.

Question 4: In my free time, I prefer to:

- A: Work on my creative projects or hobbies.
- B: Enjoy simple pleasures and relax.
- C: Read, study, or engage in thoughtful discussion.
- D: Travel, explore, or try something new.
- E: Fight for a cause I believe in or challenge myself.
- F: Experiment with new ideas or work on personal development.
- G: Train for a competition or set a new personal record.
- H: Spend quality time with my partner or close friends.
- I: Play games, tell jokes, or entertain.
- J: Hang out with family and friends, enjoying familiar activities.
- K: Volunteer or help someone out.
- L: Organize my life or plan future goals.

Question 5: The motto I resonate with most is:

- A: "Art is the lie that reveals the truth." - Pablo Picasso
- B: "Simplicity is the ultimate sophistication." - Leonardo da Vinci
- C: "Knowledge speaks, but wisdom listens." - Jimi Hendrix
- D: "Not all those who wander are lost." - J.R.R. Tolkien
- E: "Rules are made to be broken."
- F: "The true sign of intelligence is not knowledge but imagination." - Albert Einstein
- G: "Where there is a will, there is a way."
- H: "Love conquers all."

- I: "Laughter is the best medicine."
- J: "Honesty is the best policy."
- K: "Care for those who are ignored by others."
- L: "Lead, follow, or get out of the way." - Thomas Paine

Question 6: When making decisions:

- A: I rely on my creativity and what feels unique.
- B: I choose what seems to bring the most harmony and happiness.
- C: I look for the most logical and informed choice.
- D: I choose the option that offers the most freedom and adventure.
- E: I don't shy away from the unconventional or provocative choice.
- F: I consider the most transformative and impactful outcome.
- G: I stand by what is brave and challenging.
- H: I prioritize what will strengthen my relationships.
- I: I choose whatever will be the most fun or bring the most joy.
- J: I opt for the most realistic and dependable path.
- K: I focus on the choice that allows me to support and care for others.
- L: I seek to establish control and order with my decision.

Question 7: My ideal work environment is one where:

- A: I can create and innovate.
- B: There is a sense of community and positivity.
- C: Knowledge and wisdom are valued above all.
- D: I have the autonomy to explore and experiment.

- E: I can challenge the status quo and make a statement.
- F: Transformation and change are at the forefront.
- G: Courage and action are recognized and rewarded.
- H: Relationships and connections are nurtured.
- I: Humor and play are part of the daily routine.
- J: Everyone is treated with equality and respect.
- K: I can make a real difference in people's lives.
- L: Leadership and decisive action drive success.

Question 8: In a crisis, I am:

- A: The one coming up with creative solutions.
- B: The optimist who believes everything will be alright.
- C: The advisor who offers wisdom.
- D: The scout who finds the best way forward.
- E: The rebel who breaks the rules to solve the problem.
- F: The visionary who sees opportunities for change.
- G: The protector who faces danger head-on.
- H: The caregiver who ensures everyone is okay emotionally.
- I: The light-hearted one who tries to keep spirits high.
- J: The anchor who remains steady and reliable.
- K: The supporter who looks after others' needs.
- L: The leader who takes control of the situation.

Question 9: When it comes to learning:

- A: I prefer subjects that allow for self-expression and creativity.
- B: I enjoy learning about ideals, virtues, and ethics.
- C: I am drawn to philosophy, history, and the pursuit of knowledge.

- D: I love to discover new cultures, places, and ideas.
- E: I like to learn about revolutionary ideas and radical changes.
- F: I am fascinated by mysteries, symbols, and the unknown.
- G: I am interested in strategies, tactics, and self-discipline.
- H: I focus on human relationships and emotional intelligence.
- I: I look for things that are entertaining and enjoyable.
- J: I value practical skills and real-world applications.
- K: I am moved by studies about care, compassion, and community.
- L: I am attracted to leadership, management, and organizational theories.

Question 10: In my social circle:

- A: I am seen as the imaginative and original one.
- B: I am considered innocent and trustworthy.
- C: I am known as knowledgeable and reflective.
- D: I am an adventurous and independent spirit.
- E: I am the one who challenges and provokes thought.
- F: I am the problem solver and the change-maker.
- G: I am the brave one who stands up for everyone.
- H: I am a passionate and devoted friend or partner.
- I: I am playful and light-hearted.
- J: I am reliable and honest.
- K: I am a nurturing and caring presence.
- L: I am the natural leader and decision-maker.

Question 11: My approach to life is mostly about:

- A: Finding beauty and creating art in the world around me.
- B: Maintaining innocence and belief in the good.
- C: Seeking truth and deeper understanding.
- D: Seeking adventure and new experiences.
- E: Defying conventions and embracing freedom.
- F: Transforming realities and manifesting possibilities.
- G: Being courageous and taking on challenges.
- H: Building and nurturing meaningful relationships.
- I: Enjoying life and not taking things too seriously.
- J: Being grounded and valuing simplicity.
- K: Caring for others and offering help wherever needed.
- L: Leading by example and establishing a clear vision.

Question 12. My ideal work environment is one where I can:

- A: Be artistic and not constrained by too many rules.
- B: Feel secure and know that I'm making a positive impact.
- C: Constantly learn and apply knowledge.
- D: Have autonomy and face new challenges regularly.
- E: Challenge the way things are and propose new ideas.
- F: Innovate and work on projects that change people's lives.
- G: Lead by example, tackle complex tasks, and inspire others.
- H: Foster deep connections and work in a team-oriented environment.
- I: Have fun, encourage a joyful atmosphere, and not take things too seriously.

- J: Provide reliable support and have clear expectations.
- K: Offer support to my colleagues where it's most needed.
- L: Direct operations and make strategic decisions.

Scoring

After completing the quiz, tally the number of times you chose each letter corresponding to the questions. The letter with the highest count indicates your dominant archetype. If there's a tie or a close second, it suggests you may share characteristics with multiple archetypes–which is common as people are complex and multifaceted. In the case where you have more than one dominant archetype, read up on both.

The Artist

Shadow Side: The Artist's Shadow may manifest as being overly perfectionistic or self-indulgent, avoiding practical concerns in favor of artistic ones, or being prone to mood swings and sensitivity to criticism.

Illuminated Side: When illuminated, The Artist is a visionary, able to create and inspire with originality and a deep connection to their work, uplifting others with their creativity.

The Innocent

Shadow Side: The Innocent may be naive, allowing others to take advantage, or become overly dependent on people for security and well-being.

Illuminated Side: In its illuminated form, The Innocent sees the world with wonder and optimism, promoting positivity, and offering hope to others.

The Sage

Shadow Side: The Sage's Shadow might emerge as overly critical or dogmatic, possibly indulging in intellectual superiority or analysis paralysis.

Illuminated Side: The illuminated Sage uses wisdom and insight to guide others, fostering enlightenment and understanding through their pursuit of knowledge.

The Explorer

Shadow Side: The Explorer could become restless to the point of perpetual dissatisfaction or might avoid commitment and deep connections in favor of constant change.

Illuminated Side: When illuminated, The Explorer embodies independence and courage, inspiring others to find their path and embrace life's journey.

The Outlaw

Shadow Side: The Outlaw's Shadow may reveal itself as destructiveness or a penchant for chaos, rejecting any form of authority to the detriment of self and others.

Illuminated Side: The illuminated Outlaw challenges the status quo to bring about positive change, breaking through barriers to create new ways of thinking and being.

The Magician

Shadow Side: The Magician's Shadow can lead to manipulation or deceit, using charisma for selfish ends, or becoming disconnected from reality.

Illuminated Side: In its best form, The Magician is transformative, facilitating growth and realizing visions that benefit the greater good.

The Hero

Shadow Side: The Hero may become arrogant or overly aggressive, engaging in conflicts needlessly or taking on challenges to feed their ego.

Illuminated Side: The illuminated Hero is brave and determined, using their strength to protect, inspire, and lead by example.

The Lover

Shadow Side: The Lover's Shadow might result in possessiveness, jealousy, or a need for approval that can lead to self-abandonment.

Illuminated Side: When illuminated, The Lover is passionate and genuine, fostering deep connections and celebrating the beauty in relationships.

The Jester

Shadow Side: The Jester could devolve into frivolity or irresponsibility, using humor to deflect from deeper issues or to avoid serious commitment.

Illuminated Side: The illuminated Jester brings joy and laughter, helping others see the lighter side of life and embracing the moment.

The Everyman/Woman

Shadow Side: The Everyman/Everywoman might become too conformist or lose their sense of self in an effort to belong, leading to a lack of authenticity.

Illuminated Side: In its best expression, The Everyman/Everywoman is relatable and genuine, creating a sense of community and shared human experience.

The Caregiver

Shadow Side: The Caregiver's Shadow can manifest in martyrdom or co-dependency, giving to the point of depletion or enabling negative behaviors in others.

Illuminated Side: The illuminated Caregiver is generous, selfless and supportive, providing strength and care without losing themselves in the process.

The Ruler

Shadow Side: The Ruler may become tyrannical or controlling, obsessed with order and power, and lacking empathy for those they lead.

Illuminated Side: When illuminated, The Ruler is a responsible and fair leader, using their authority to create and maintain a prosperous and just environment.

Each archetype has its strengths and weaknesses, and recognising your dominant archetype can offer insights into your behavior and motivations. This awareness can guide you towards personal growth, helping you leverage your strengths and work on areas that may need development. Remember, it's common to see yourself in multiple archetypes, reflecting the complexity of your personality.

TO KNOW YOURSELF IS TO LOVE YOURSELF - DREAM READING FOR INSIGHT

Dreams were central to Carl Jung's work because he believed they provided a direct portal to the unconscious mind. Jung saw dreams as invaluable tools in the psychotherapeutic process, offering insights into our innermost thoughts, desires, and fears. Unlike his contemporary, Sigmund Freud, who interpreted dreams primarily as expressions of repressed sexual and aggressive urges, Jung viewed dreams as meaningful sources of symbolic messages aimed at resolving psychological imbalances and guiding the process of individuation—the path to the integrated self.

Jung believed dreams use symbolic language and imagery to communicate messages from the unconscious to the conscious mind. These symbols are not arbitrary but universal archetypes that carry specific meanings. Through dreams, the unconscious expresses unresolved issues, offers solutions, and provides a compensatory balance to the dreamer's conscious attitude. In this way, dreams powerfully reveal aspects of the Shadow and allow you to open the doorway to becoming your own ***Oracle.***

> *"This whole creation is essentially subjective, and the dream is the theatre where the dreamer is at once: scene, actor, prompter, stage manager, author, audience, and critic."*
>
> — CARL JUNG

Shadow-Like Dream Symbols

- **Dark Figures or Shadows:** Often represent the unknown or unacknowledged parts of oneself.
- **Monsters or Threatening Animals:** Symbolize primal fears, repressed emotions, or uncontrolled impulses.
- **Chase Dreams:** Being chased can indicate avoidance of confronting an issue or aspect of oneself.
- **Conflict or Violence:** Reflects internal struggles or unacknowledged anger.
- **Being Trapped or Imprisoned:** Suggests feelings of restriction, perhaps self-imposed, or aspects of life where one feels confined.
- **Lost or Searching for Something:** This can indicate a lost aspect of the self or an ongoing search for identity and meaning.
- **Falling:** Often symbolizes a loss of control, fear of failure, or surrendering to unconscious processes.
- **Being Naked in Public:** Reveals vulnerability, shame, or hidden aspects of oneself that one fears exposing.
- **Malfunctioning Devices or Vehicles:** These may represent feelings of inadequacy or a lack of control over one's direction in life.
- **Dilapidated Houses or Buildings:** Often symbolize neglected aspects of the self or underdeveloped potential.
- **Natural Disasters:** Floods, earthquakes, or storms can symbolize overwhelming emotions or unconscious upheavals.
- **Snake:** A classic symbol for transformation, healing, or the shadowy aspects of the self, especially those related to instinctual drives.

- **Dark Alleys or Unknown Paths:** Represent the unknown journey into the depths of the self.
- **Mirrors:** Can reflect the true self, including aspects one might be ignoring or unaware of.
- **Death or Dying:** Often not a literal symbol, but rather indicative of change, the end of something, or transformation.
- **Injured or Sick Persons:** May symbolize neglected or hurt parts of oneself.
- **Toilets and Excretion:** Often deal with the release of repressed emotions or the need to eliminate harmful thoughts or feelings.
- **Adultery or Sexual Encounters:** Can represent unfulfilled desires or aspects of one's identity seeking expression.
- **Water:** Symbolizes the unconscious mind, emotions, and the flow of psychic energy. It can represent purification, renewal, or being overwhelmed by emotions.
- **Tree:** Symbolizes growth, development, and the connection between the conscious and unconscious. It can also represent life's cycles and personal growth.
- **Child:** A child represents something new, innocent, or vulnerable within the self. It can also symbolize potential for growth or aspects of the self that need nurturing.
- **House:** The house often represents the self or the psyche, with different rooms reflecting different aspects of the individual's personality or life.
- **Mountains:** Symbolize obstacles, challenges to be overcome, or high aspirations and goals.
- **Animals:** Represent instinctual aspects of the self, natural wisdom, or qualities we associate with the particular animal.

- **Vehicles:** Can symbolize how we navigate our lives or the path we are on. The condition and control of the car are important to its interpretation.
- **Roads:** Represent the journey of life or the path the individual is on, including choices and directions.
- **Bridges:** Symbolize transitions, overcoming obstacles, or connecting different aspects of the individual's life or self.
- **Clocks And Watches:** Represent the passage of time, life cycles, or deadlines and pressures.
- **Flying:** Can represent freedom, escape, or overcoming limitations and obstacles.
- **Clothes:** Symbolize the persona or how we present ourselves to the world. Different outfits can reflect different roles or identities.
- **Fire:** Represents transformation, passion, or destruction. It can symbolize the need to destroy old forms to make way for the new.
- **Gold:** Often symbolizes something valuable within the self, wisdom, or spiritual rewards.
- **Darkness:** Can represent the unknown, unconscious, or aspects of the self or life that are hidden or unclear.
- **Light:** Symbolizes consciousness, enlightenment, or understanding and clarity.
- **Keys:** Represent access, solutions, or the means to unlock something previously inaccessible or unknown.
- **Door:** This can symbolize new opportunities, transitions, or barriers depending on the context of the dream.
- **Books:** Symbolize knowledge, wisdom, or the search for understanding.
- **Food:** Can represent emotional or spiritual nourishment, or lack thereof. Specific foods may have additional meanings.

- **Ring:** The ring symbolizes commitment, unity, or completeness. In Jung's psychology, it can also represent the Self.
- **Garden:** Represents the natural, cultivated aspects of the psyche or personal growth and development.
- **Flood:** Symbolizes overwhelming emotions or situations, overwhelming unconscious forces, or a need for cleansing.
- **Crossroads:** Represent decisions, life changes, or the need to choose a direction.

Dream analysis in Jungian therapy is highly individualized, as the meaning of symbols can vary significantly depending on the dreamer's personal experiences, cultural background, and current life circumstances. The interpretation of dreams and their symbols is a nuanced process, which aims to bring unconscious content into conscious awareness and integrate it.

Weaving together the elements of a dream into a coherent narrative that provides self-insight is a process that can help you understand their unconscious motivations, fears, desires, and overall psychological state.

Becoming the interpreter of your own dreams, or even the dreams of others, in other words, an Oracle, is one of the most powerful gifts of Shadow Work. Because dreams are filled with enigmatic, elusive and often mysterious symbols, metaphors, images and messages, it's impossible to become adept at reading them without walking on the dark side with your Shadow, or the Shadow-self of the person whose dream you're aiming to read.

Dreams are a gateway to stepping into the power of becoming an Oracle. If this kind of psychic work lights your fire, I urge you to read as much as you can about dreams, or if you want to go the extra mile, begin work with a Jungian analyst trained in the art of dreamwork.

DREAM READING AND INTERPRETATION

Understanding the Symbolism

1. **Personal and Collective Unconscious:** Dreams arise from the individual unconscious (repressed memories and experiences) and the collective unconscious (universal symbols shared among all humans). Recognize that some symbols are unique to you while others belong to humanity's shared heritage.
2. **Archetypes:** Central to Jungian dream analysis are archetypes—universal, primordial images and themes that recur across cultures. Common archetypes include the Hero, the Maiden, the Shadow, the Anima/Animus, and the Self. Identify these archetypes in your dreams to uncover deeper layers of meaning.
3. **Amplification:** This technique explores a dream symbol by relating it to myths, literature, and cultural stories. Amplification helps expand the personal significance of a symbol by connecting it to its broader, universal context.

Engaging with the Dream

1. Active Imagination: A method to dialogue with dream figures and symbols, allowing them to reveal their meanings. Sit quietly, revisit the dream, and let your imagination interact with the images. Ask questions and listen to the responses, treating dream characters as real entities within your psyche.

- **What emotions and sensations do I experience when I visualize this dream image or scenario?**

  Understanding the emotional and physical responses can provide insights into the underlying issues or themes the dream is addressing.

- **What does this dream character or symbol want to tell me?**

  Engaging in a dialogue with dream figures can help uncover hidden messages or aspects of your psyche.

- **How does this dream scene relate to my current life situation or personal challenges?**

  Connecting the dream content to your waking life can help identify patterns or unresolved issues.

- **What would happen if I changed an element of this dream?**

  Experimenting with different scenarios can reveal new perspectives and solutions.

- **What do I fear or resist in this dream, and why?**

  Exploring fears and resistances can lead to deeper self-understanding and personal growth.

2. **The Living Symbol**: Jung believed that symbols are alive and dynamic. Rather than seeking a fixed interpretation, engage with

the symbol as an evolving entity that changes over time. Pay attention to how the symbol's meaning shifts with your personal growth and experiences.

Integrating the Dream

1. **Anima and Animus:** Dreams often reveal the Anima (the feminine aspect in men) or Animus (the masculine aspect in women). Engaging with these inner figures can balance the feminine and masculine energies within you, fostering psychological harmony.
2. **Individuation:** The ultimate goal of Jungian dream analysis is individuation—the process of becoming your true self. Dreams guide you on this path, highlighting areas where you need to grow, heal, or change. Reflect on how your dreams align with your waking life and the person you are becoming.

Practical Steps

1. **Dream Journal:** Keep a journal by your bedside and write down your dreams immediately upon waking. Record every detail, no matter how trivial it seems. Over time, patterns and themes will emerge, offering insights into your unconscious mind.
2. **Reflect and Relate:** Spend time reflecting on your dreams and relating them to your daily life. Consider how dream symbols and narratives resonate with your current experiences, emotions, and challenges.
3. **Seek Guidance:** Sometimes, dreams can be complex and difficult to interpret on your own. Seek guidance from a

Jungian analyst or a therapist trained in dream analysis to gain deeper insights and support.

4. **Identify Key Symbols:** Highlight the main symbols that appear in your dream. These could be objects, characters, animals, or even actions that carry a significant weight in the narrative.
5. **Explore Personal Associations:** For each symbol, jot down your personal associations and feelings. What does each symbol mean to you personally? Avoid relying solely on generic interpretations.
6. **Consider the Emotions:** Reflect on the emotions you experienced during the dream and upon waking. How do these emotions relate to your current life situation?
7. **Analyze the Setting and Context:** Look at where the dream takes place and the context around each symbol or action. Settings can offer insights into your state of mind or areas of your life that are being highlighted.
8. **Identify the Plot:** Try to discern a beginning, middle, and end within your dream. This narrative structure can reveal the underlying issues or conflicts in the dream.
9. **Look for Recurring Themes or Symbols:** If you notice specific themes or symbols appearing in multiple dreams, they may represent ongoing or unresolved issues in your life.
10. **Connect to Life Events:** Consider how the dream reflects your waking life. Are there situations, relationships, or feelings that resonate with the dream's content?
11. **Consult with Others:** Sometimes , discussing the dream with someone else can offer fresh perspectives and insights that you might not have considered. Or you could hunt online for a dream group via Facebook or one of the Jungian societies all over the world.

12. **Reflect on Potential Messages:** After analyzing the dream, think about what messages or insights it might be offering. How can these insights be applied to your growth or current life circumstances?

Types of Dreams

- **Lucid Dreams:** Dreams where the dreamer is aware they are dreaming and can sometimes influence the dream's outcome.
- **Nightmares:** Disturbing dreams that can cause feelings of fear, stress, or anxiety, often reflecting underlying emotional issues.
- **Recurring Dreams:** Dreams that repeat themselves, either exactly or with slight variations, which may indicate unresolved conflicts or stresses.
- **Prophetic Dreams:** Also known as precognitive dreams, these are dreams that seemingly predict future events. While scientifically controversial, they are a significant part of many cultural narratives.
- **Healing Dreams:** Dreams that provide insight into health or emotional healing, sometimes offering solutions to problems or relief from emotional distress.
- **Vivid Dreams:** Extremely clear and lifelike dreams often remembered in great detail.
- **Waking Dreams:** States of daydreaming where the mind wanders to a dream-like narrative while the individual is awake, often blending imagination with feelings and desires.
- **Symbolic Dreams:** Dreams that are rich in symbols and archetypal images, offering deep insights into the unconscious mind , according to Jungian psychology.

- **Visitation Dreams:** Dreams where the dreamer encounters deceased loved ones or significant figures, often feeling as if the visitation carries a message or a sense of real interaction.

Each type of dream offers a unique window into your subconscious mind, providing valuable insights into your inner world, concerns, and aspirations.

Interpreting and reading dreams through a Jungian perspective is a rich, transformative practice. By engaging with the symbols, archetypes, and narratives of your dreams, you embark on a journey of self-discovery and healing. Dreams are not mere fragments of the night; they are profound messages from the unconscious, guiding you towards wholeness and individuation. Dreams offer a free ticket to liberation as you transform to become the Oracle. Embrace this journey with curiosity and openness and allow your dreams to illuminate the path to your true self.

THE QUEST FOR LIGHT - A HEROIC UNIVERSAL STORY

The Descent

In the history of human mythos, the journey into the underworld is a powerful motif that symbolizes the descent into the deepest realms of the psyche, a foundational element of the Hero's Journey that professor in mythology and comparative religion Joseph Campbell meticulously detailed in his seminal work "The Hero with a Thousand Faces." This archetypal voyage echoes across virtually every human storytelling tradition and is prominent in Egyptian, Greek and Roman mythology. It also aligns profoundly with Carl Jung's concept of delving into the collective unconscious to confront, and eventually integrate, the Shadow within.

I'm going to take a little time to explain these myths because they point the way for our descent into the inky darkness of our unconscious selves and the gifts that are bestowed when we undertake this quest.

The myth of Hades, the Greek god of the underworld, encapsulates this descent. Hades reigns over the place where souls journey after death, representing a realm of deep reflection and transformation. The hero's descent into Hades is symbolic of a confrontation with the most repressed parts of the self—the Shadow. This encounter is essential for any true transformation, as it is in the depths where one uncovers truth and gains wisdom.

According to Greek mythology, Hades is the enigmatic ruler of the underworld, a realm cloaked in shadows and mystery. Born of Cronus and Rhea, Hades, along with his brothers Zeus and Poseidon, carved out their dominions: the sky, the sea, and the depths of the earth.

Hades' tale intertwines fate and love, beginning with the abduction of Persephone, the radiant daughter of Demeter, goddess of the harvest. Struck by her beauty, Hades emerged from his shadowy realm, determined to make her his queen. One day, as Persephone gathered flowers in a meadow, the earth beneath her feet split open, and Hades swept her away to his underground kingdom.

Despair gripped Demeter, casting the earth into a barren winter as she mourned the loss of her daughter. The world, once vibrant and fecund, turned cold and lifeless. Driven by love and desperation, Demeter's plight reached Zeus, who intervened to broker a deal.

A compromise was struck. Persephone would spend part of the year with Hades in the underworld and the remainder with her mother on the earth's surface. Thus, the cycle of seasons was born. When Persephone returns to Demeter, the earth blooms with the promise of spring and summer, and when she descends to Hades, autumn and winter follow, reflecting Demeter's sorrow.

Hades, often misunderstood, is not a figure of malice but one of balance and certainty. His love for Persephone is profound, adding depth to his character as more than just a ruler of the dead. Together, they reign over the underworld, embodying the intricate dance of life, death, and rebirth that shapes the world above.

Similarly, the myth of Pandora's Box illustrates the unleashing of unseen shadows upon the world. When Pandora opens the forbidden container, she releases all the hidden ills of humanity, much like when we release the repressed and ignored aspects of our personality–it can be ugly and scary when the evils get out of the box. Yet, the myth also speaks of hope, suggesting that even in exploring our darkest corners, there's potential for redemption and growth.

Created by the gods themselves, Pandora was a being of unparalleled beauty and grace, crafted from clay by Hephaestus and endowed with gifts from each deity. Zeus, the king of the gods, had a special plan for her—a plan that would forever alter the human world.

Pandora was given a box, a beautiful container with intricate designs glimmering with divine craftsmanship. However, she was also given a stern warning: she should never open it. This seemingly innocuous box held a profound secret—a secret Zeus intended to unleash upon humanity.

Curiosity, one of the gifts bestowed upon Pandora, gnawed relentlessly at her, and the box whispered a siren call she couldn't resist. One fateful day, unable to bear the suspense any longer, Pandora lifted the lid. In an instant, the world was transformed.

All the evils and miseries that plague humanity issued forth from the box: sickness, sorrow, jealousy, loss, greed, and despair. Once released, these dark forces spread swiftly across the earth, inflicting pain and suffering on humankind. Pandora, horrified by what she had unleashed, tried desperately to close the box, but it was too late.

Yet, amid the chaos, a glimmer of light remained within the box. It was Hope, the last and most precious gift. Although overshadowed by all the unleashed evils, Hope stayed behind, offering a beacon of light in even the darkest times. This final gift ensured that humanity would always have something to cling to, no matter how dire their circumstances.

Like the Greeks and Romans before them, Campbell and Jung understood these myths not as literal tales but as metaphoric expressions of the inner workings of the human spirit. The collective unconscious holds the heritage of human myths, emotions, and archetypes. The hero's journey into this abyss is a profound psychological pilgrimage. It is here, in the confrontation with the Shadow, that we aim to reconcile with those aspects of the self that are out of balance or in opposition.

Through this reconciliation, the hero emerges transformed, often as a bearer of light or wisdom, much like Persephone does in the Hades myth, who emerges from the underworld each spring–symbolising rebirth and new beginnings. This light is not just for personal edification; it is a torch to light the way for others.

The hero, having faced the darkest paths within the labyrinth of their unconscious, emerges as the integrated self—no longer just a warrior of the light but also a guardian of the darkness. This integration represents the true power of the hero's journey.

Initiating yourself into these mysteries is a path for heroes and heroines. You emerge stronger and wiser. The gift of all these heroic tasks is the integration of your being, the unification of your Light and Shadow, and gives you access to the high priest/priestess within–your inner Oracle.

Emerging From the Descent with The Elixir

In the archetypal narrative of the Hero's Journey, the final act is "The Return with The Elixir," a phase where the hero comes back from the underworld, or from his transformative journey, not just with new insights for personal growth but with gifts that benefit society at large, (for example, when Persephone returns from the underworld she brings springtime with her). This is the point at which the individual journey transcends personal transformation and assumes a collective significance.

Joseph Campbell, in "The Hero with a Thousand Faces," articulates this when he writes, “The hero comes back from this mysterious adventure with the power to bestow boons on his fellow man.” The ‘elixir’ can be literal or metaphorical—it may be a secret, a treasure, or even a new perspective or wisdom, but its essence is that it has the potential to heal, enlighten, and transform not just the hero but the world.

Greek and Roman myths are full of such returns. In Greek mythology, Asclepius, the god of healing, is said to have journeyed to the underworld.

On his return, he brought back knowledge that could resurrect the dead, serving humanity with the gift of medicine. In Roman mythology, Aeneas's visit to the underworld in Virgil's "Aeneid" gives him the knowledge and resolve necessary to found the city of

Rome. These myths tell us that the path to the Shadow bestows healing and medicine as well as wisdom and resilience.

Jung's concept of individuation encompasses this heroic return. Jung posits that a person who has successfully navigated the depths of the unconscious and integrated their Shadow emerges with a sense of completeness and a vision that transcends personal ego. In "The Structure and Dynamics of the Psyche," Jung says, "The bringing back of the treasure hard to attain is the realization of the self."

The return with the elixir is a metaphor for imparting the wisdom gained from the encounter with the Shadow, the treasure from the dark realms to society. It's about disseminating newfound knowledge, healing, or insight, which contributes to the evolution of collective consciousness. Jung's model implies that the hero, upon returning, has a moral imperative to use his gifts for the greater good. By doing so, the hero bridges the personal and the collective, between the unconscious depths and conscious reality.

This return doesn't have to be a grand gesture; it can be as subtle as a change in how one interacts with others or contributes to their community. The hero, now the master of two worlds—the inner world of the psyche and the outer social world—must share the wisdom and embody the change they wish to see.

My own close encounters with the Shadow tell me that the journey into the Shadowlands is, therefore, not just a personal quest but a societal one. It encourages us to bring back what we have learned to heal, uplift, and enlighten our friends, our loved ones, and the society we live in and share.

ARCHETYPES AND YOUR INNER ORACLE

In your own Hades world, your hidden paradise where the Shadow reigns supreme, the journey towards becoming your own Oracle begins with the profound process of uniting the light and dark aspects of yourself. This union is the essence of Shadow Work—the path that leads to the integration of all parts of the psyche—bestowing wisdom, self-acceptance, self-love and personal transformation.

At the heart of this journey lies the understanding of our archetypes, those universal symbols and motifs embedded within our collective unconscious. These are brought to consciousness through the rich narratives of our dreams and waking imaginings.

These dreams, messages, intuitions, feelings, gut sensations, waking dreams, and insights gained through divination tools such as tarot, angel cards, I Ching, clairaudience and clairvoyance ARE our Oracle speaking to us.

The art here is to tune into the messages (or Oracles), so you may transform into the bearer of those Oracles and become the very creature that speaks that wisdom to the world—and yourself.

Carl Jung revealed that these archetypes—like the Shadow, the Anima/Animus, the Self, the Oracle and the Hero—serve as guiding forces in our psychological development. They manifest in our dreams, behaviors and fantasies, offering us clues to the hidden parts of our unconscious selves.

If you want to transform yourself into the Oracle and avail yourself of its magic and power, you can't just click your heels and wish yourself home like Dorothy did in the Wizard of Oz. Becoming the Oracle requires an initiation. In this case, it doesn't demand a blood sacrifice, donning robes and joining a monastic order, or any real sacrifice. What it does require, however, is the courage to go deep into your personal underworld and be prepared to gather the messages you're given there. Those messages may come in the form of archetypes, dream symbols, waking visions, whispers of a profound nature, like clairaudient transmissions or even clairvoyance itself—where you really do tap into the universal unconscious and return with vital wisdom and even visions of the future.

It takes guts. It takes intention. But most of all, it takes openness, and a full and reverent acceptance of whatever mystical message comes to you. This is solemn work, and it's your sacred duty as an initiate of this mystery tradition to protect it.

Dreams, often referred to as the royal road to the unconscious, provide a vivid storybook of symbols and narratives that reflect our inner lives. By keeping a detailed dream journal and regularly recording our dreams, we see recurring themes and symbols that align with archetypal patterns. These dreams are not mere fragments of our imagination; they are messages from the Oracle of our soul, emanating from the depths of our unconscious, guiding us towards self-discovery and integration.

Another way to tap into the power of the Oracle is through active imagination. It allows you to engage deeply and directly in a dialogue with these dream figures, revealing concealed meanings and insights. Visualizing conversations with these characters and allowing them to speak can unveil profound truths about who we really are. This is Oracle Work. This method, a fast track to communicating with the wisdom within, reveals the dynamic interplay between the different parts of our psyche and how they function in our lives.

As we unite our dark and light aspects, we create a bridge so the Oracle may meet us where we are. In listening to its messages, longings, whispers, predictions and divinations, we cultivate a deep sense of self-awareness and acceptance. But most importantly, this bridge offers us a path to use the wisdom we've gained for the benefit of ourselves and the upliftment of others. The mere act of listening to the wisdom offered up, without judgement or editing, transforms us into the Oracle—the source of inner wisdom and guidance. The Oracle, in this sense, is both the message and the messenger—a polestar of self-awareness that navigates life with clarity and authenticity.

Shadow Work and Oracle Work require courage and honesty. They involve facing the parts of ourselves we'd rather ignore and messages we'd, sometimes, rather not hear. This deep listening and integration process unfolds through acknowledgment and compassion.

Are you ready to reveal who you really are to the world?

You are the Oracle.

CHAPTER FIVE

SHADOW AND RELATIONSHIPS

Far from being a formula for loneliness and isolation, recognizing and integrating our Shadow promises a path towards authentic, profound connections with others. It teaches us that by facing our innermost selves, we may unlock the door to more profound empathy, more genuine relationships, and a liberating acceptance of not just who we are but who we have the potential to become.

As we deep-dive into the intricate interplay between our Shadows and our relationships, let's grab this opportunity to shed light on our unexplored depths, transforming our touchstones with others into reservoirs of growth, healing, and unconditional love.

Together, let's discover how the courageous act of facing our darkness can light the way to the essence of true friendship, camaraderie, kinship and love—where hearts meet, understandings deepen, and spirits rise.

The serendipitous by-product of all this investigation is that by opening your heart to others and allowing yourself to give more love and light, you make more space for self-love and self-acceptance.

So go for it! Let in more light and become a lantern for everyone else in your life.

Our Shadows don't just affect us; they influence our relationships with everyone we meet. This chapter explores how your Shadow shapes your interactions and perceptions in relationships. Through discovering your Attachment Style, reflective writing prompts, Socratic questions and a powerful Self-Love Mindfulness exercise, you'll gain valuable insights into how your unconscious parts play out in your interactions with others.

> *"I will love the light for it shows me the way, yet I will endure the darkness because it shows me the stars."*
>
> — OG MANDINO

There are many theories about why we bond with other humans. Sociologists, evolutionary biologists and anthropologists suggest it's mainly for survival. Members of the group who display antisocial or dangerous behaviours can find themselves cast out. And, if you relied on the group for food and shelter, as has been the case for much of humankind's history, then being in the "out-group" can mean death. In modern Western societies, being "out" usually leads to loneliness and isolation–which also has health consequences, as loneliness is worse for your health than smoking or obesity.

British psychiatrist John Bowlby formed a hypothesis that has gained traction over the past few years called "Attachment Theory". He believed that most baby animals need to form consistent and intimate bonds with their "primary caregivers", usually the mother; however, it can also be any other person intimately involved with a child in babyhood. He posited that once attached, babies become depressed, desperate and disturbed if they're separated from that intimate person.

He found that when infants are separated from their mothers, they respond in predictable ways: They protest loudly and search frantically for their mothers and become sad, passive, and despairing when they can't find her. Bowlby studied these responses for over twenty years and found many parallels between disturbed adults and broken attachments in childhood. Furthermore, Bowlby believed that early relationships with caregivers influence social relationships throughout life. His theory suggests that secure attachment to a caregiver provides a child with a sense of safety and security–necessary for exploring the environment and learning. Bowlby identified four stages of attachment: ***Pre-attachment, attachment-in-the-making, clear-cut attachment, and formation of reciprocal relationships.***

ATTACHMENT STYLES

Bowlby's theory was further developed by his colleague Mary Ainsworth, who identified three primary attachment styles through the "Strange Situation" study: secure, anxious-ambivalent (also known as anxious-resistant), and avoidant. Later, researchers Main and Solomon added a fourth style, disorganized attachment.

Secure Attachment

People with a secure attachment style tend to have healthy, trusting relationships. They are comfortable with intimacy and independence and balance the two. Securely attached individuals are often empathetic and supportive partners, capable of seeking and providing comfort when needed.

Anxious-Ambivalent Attachment

Those with an anxious-ambivalent attachment style often feel insecure about their relationships. They may worry that their partner does not love them or might leave them, leading to clinginess or dependency. This attachment style can result in high levels of emotional expressiveness, anxiety, and impulsiveness in relationships.

Avoidant Attachment

Individuals with an avoidant attachment style tend to be emotionally distant from their partners. They may struggle with intimacy and prioritize independence and self-sufficiency. Their reluctance to depend on others or open up can challenge the development of close, intimate relationships.

Disorganized Attachment

A lack of clear attachment behavior characterizes disorganized attachment. This style can emerge from a background of trauma or abuse and is often marked by contradictory and erratic behaviors and confusion about relationships. People with disorganized attachment may struggle to form stable, trusting relationships.

Effects on Relationships

According to Bowlby, and many other psychologists, psychiatrists and counsellors, attachment styles profoundly influence how people perceive and interact in their relationships. Those with secure attachments tend to have healthier and more satisfying relationships, while those with insecure attachments (anxious, avoidant and disorganized), may experience various challenges. Anxious people may be overly dependent and fear abandonment; avoidant individuals might struggle to connect and share with their partners, and those with disorganized attachments may find it difficult to trust and rely on their partners. Understanding one's attachment style can provide valuable insights into relationship patterns and offer pathways toward richer, more fulfilling connections.

I'm not qualified to draw a long bow and say that attachment style is directly related to Shadow, but one thing I can say is that knowledge is power. The more knowledge you have about your relationship style (whether you're avoidant, disorganised, anxious-ambivalent or secure) is a good place to begin your journey into how much of your relationships are ruled by your conscious self and how much might be ruled by your Shadow self?

Without awareness of our "stuff," we can't change. Simple. When you're aware of how you operate, you can change. You have choice, free will, and power.

QUIZ - YOUR ATTACHMENT STYLE

Instructions

Answer the following questions on a scale from 1 to 5, where 1 = strongly disagree, and 5 = strongly agree. Be as honest as possible for the most accurate assessment.

Questions

1. I find it easy to become emotionally close to others.
2. I am comfortable depending on others and having others depend on me.
3. I worry about being abandoned or someone getting too close to me.
4. I prefer not to show a partner how I feel deep down.
5. My partners often want to be more intimate than I feel comfortable being.
6. I often worry that my partner does not really love me or won't want to stay with me.
7. I find it difficult to trust others completely or to depend on them.
8. I get nervous when anyone gets too close, and often, love partners want me to be more intimate than I feel comfortable being.
9. I am comfortable sharing my deepest thoughts and feelings with my partner.
10. My desire to merge completely with my partner can scare them away.

11. I find it easy to trust others.
12. I don't feel comfortable opening up to others.
13. Being close to others is very important to me.
14. I often worry my partner will not want to keep me.
15. I can share my deepest fears and feelings with my partner.
16. I prefer not to be too close to romantic partners.
17. I often feel uncomfortable with people getting too emotionally close to me.
18. I worry a lot about my relationships.
19. When I show my feelings for someone, I'm afraid they will not feel the same about me.
20. I feel secure in my close relationships.

Scoring

Total your score for each question. The sum will indicate your primary attachment style. Higher scores on certain questions correlate to specific attachment styles, as described below:

Secure Attachment: High scores on questions 1, 2, 9, 11, 13, 15, and 20 suggest a secure attachment style. You're comfortable with intimacy and independence, balancing those two polarities in relationships. You're likely to trust your partner and maintain healthy, fulfilling relationships.

Anxious Attachment: High scores on questions 3, 6, 10, 14, 18, and 19 indicate an anxious attachment style. You may often feel insecure about your relationships and fear abandonment. You might need a lot of validation and reassurance from your partner, which can sometimes strain the relationship.

Avoidant Attachment: High scores on questions 4, 5, 7, 8, 12, 16, and 17 suggest an avoidant attachment style. You value your independence and often feel uncomfortable with too much closeness. You may struggle to open up and trust others, keeping your partner at arm's length emotionally.

Disorganised Attachment: If your scores are relatively high across the board, including the conflicting feelings of wanting closeness but fearing it, you might have a disorganised attachment style. You might find yourself in a cycle of pushing away and then desiring closeness, which can confuse you and your partner.

How to Work with Your Attachment Style

Secure Attachment

You're likely to have stable and harmonious relationships. You feel comfortable with intimacy and asking for help, and you can support your partner's independence. That said, you can still benefit from strategies to develop growth and resilience in relationships.

Strategies For Growth

Continue Emotional Openness: Keep the lines of communication open. Sharing feelings, dreams, and fears with a partner strengthens bonds.

Encourage Partner's Development: Support partners in exploring their own attachment styles and emotional growth, facilitating a deeper mutual understanding.

Maintain Independence: Ensure personal and partner's independence is maintained. Balancing intimacy with autonomy is vital to long-lasting relationships.

Anxious Attachment

You may need more reassurance and intimacy in relationships than those with other attachment styles. Awareness and communication about your needs can help build stronger, more secure relationships. Those with an anxious attachment style may experience persistent worry about their relationships' security. Their strategies should focus on building self-esteem and trust.

Strategies for Growth

Self-Soothing Techniques: Learn techniques to manage anxiety and emotional distress, such as deep breathing, meditation, or journaling.

Seek Therapy: Cognitive behavioral therapy (CBT) can help identify and challenge the thought patterns that fuel anxiety and dependence.

Communicate Needs Clearly: Instead of expecting a partner to guess your needs, openly communicate them. This requires understanding what you truly need first.

Avoidant Attachment

You might prioritize independence over intimacy, making your partner feel neglected or unimportant. Understanding your need for space and communicating it in a healthy way can improve your relationship dynamics.

Strategies For Growth

Challenge Beliefs About Independence: Recognize that needing others is not a sign of weakness and that intimacy can be rewarding.

Gradual Vulnerability: Take small steps towards opening up emotionally, seeing that vulnerability is a strength, not a weakness.

Understand Your Triggers: Identify situations or emotions that trigger the desire to pull away and explore them with a therapist to understand their roots.

Disorganised Attachment

Balancing your desire for intimacy with your fear of getting too close can be challenging. Therapy or counselling can help you understand your fears and learn how to create healthier attachment behaviours in relationships.

Strategies for Growth

Identify Fears: Reflect on past experiences that contribute to fears of intimacy and abandonment. Understanding these can help in addressing them.

Embrace Mindfulness: Mindfulness and present-moment awareness can help manage overwhelming emotions and reduce the impulse to push people away.

Professional Support: Engage in therapy, especially strategies that focus on attachment and trauma, such as Eye Movement Desensitization and Reprocessing (EMDR) or Dialectical Behavior Therapy (DBT).

Your attachment style is not a life sentence. With self-awareness, the right tools and determined work, it's possible to develop more secure attachment behaviors and improve your relationships.

Note: None of the strategies or practices outlined here are a substitute for professional medical or psychological advice.

> "There is strong shadow where there is much light."
>
> — JOHANN WOLFGANG VON GOETHE

HEALING THE WOUNDED CHILD

From a Jungian perspective, childhood stress and trauma can play a significant role in the formation of the Shadow. When a child experiences trauma, they may unconsciously choose to bury the feelings associated with that trauma deep within their psyche as a survival mechanism to avoid pain.

These repressed memories and emotions do not vanish; they become part of the Shadow. In adulthood, these unresolved issues can manifest in relationships through *projection*–where we attribute our own unacceptable traits to others. For instance, someone punished for showing anger as a child might repress this emotion in their Shadow. As an adult, they might find themselves intensely triggered by displays of anger in others or, conversely, may unknowingly provoke anger in their partners.

Healing childhood trauma in the context of Jungian psychology involves the process of *individuation,* which is the integration of the conscious and unconscious parts of the psyche, the dark and light, male and female aspects–leading to psychological maturity and wholeness.

The following steps are key to this healing process.

Step 1.

Acknowledgment

Recognizing that there are repressed parts of our psyche affecting our behavior is the first step towards healing. Without this realization, the Shadow remains hidden and powerful.

Step 2.

Engagement

This involves actively engaging with the Shadow. Techniques like dream analysis, active imagination, and expressive arts can facilitate dialogue with the unconscious.

Step 3.

Understanding

Seek to understand the origins of your Straits. Acknowledge the defensive nature of these mechanisms in childhood while exploring their maladaptive impact in adulthood.

Step 4.

Compassion

Approach your inner child with compassion rather than judgment. Healing comes from offering the understanding and kindness to oneself that the child did not receive during the traumatic events. This may involve learning how to parent yourself.

Step 5.

Transformation

Transform the energy of the Shadow from destructive to constructive through conscious awareness and choice. Traits once seen as negative can often be redirected in positive ways when recognized and integrated.

Step 6.

Integration: Incorporate the learned aspects of the Shadow into your conscious life. Accept that both light and darkness are parts of a whole, and allow yourself to express your full range of emotions and traits in healthy ways.

Healing Childhood Trauma Through Expressive Writing

Childhood trauma can leave lasting scars on us, affecting our mental and physical health well into adulthood. However, emerging research suggests that expressive writing can be a powerful tool in the healing process. By putting thoughts and emotions into words, we can confront and make sense of our experiences, leading to profound psychological and physiological changes.

Expressive Writing and Trauma

Expressive writing is writing about one's deepest thoughts and feelings surrounding a traumatic experience. This process allows us to explore our emotions in a safe and controlled way without fear of judgment or repercussions. When it comes to childhood trauma, expressive writing can be particularly beneficial, as it provides an opportunity to revisit and reframe past events in a new light.

Numerous studies have demonstrated the effectiveness of expressive writing in healing childhood trauma. For example, a meta-analysis published in the journal "Psychological Bulletin" in 2017 reviewed 146 studies and found that expressive writing interventions led to significant improvements in psychological well-being, including reductions in symptoms of depression and anxiety.

Another study, conducted by Smyth et al. (2019) and published in "Health Psychology," explored the physiological effects of expressive writing on people with a history of childhood trauma. The researchers found that participants who engaged in expressive writing experienced lower levels of stress hormones, such as cortisol, and showed improvements in immune function compared to those in a control group.

The mechanisms underlying the healing effects of expressive writing on childhood trauma are multifaceted. Writing about traumatic experiences can help us make sense of our emotions, gain perspective, and develop a coherent narrative of the past. This process of "cognitive restructuring", a Cognitive Behavioral Therapy technique, can alleviate feelings of shame, guilt, and helplessness associated with childhood trauma.

Healing childhood trauma can be a complex and challenging journey and is often best guided by a professional counsellor or therapist, but expressive writing offers a promising avenue for recovery. By providing a platform for self-expression and reflection, expressive writing can empower you to confront your past, promote emotional healing, and boost well-being.

Here are some tips on how to do it:

- **Write Freely:** There are no rules or restrictions when it comes to expressive writing. Let your thoughts flow freely onto the page without worrying about grammar, spelling, or punctuation. Write as if no one else will read it. Some techniques say writing for 15-20 continuous minutes daily for 4 consecutive days can be a useful stand-alone tool.
- **Explore Your Emotions:** Allow yourself to delve into your emotions surrounding the childhood trauma. Write

about how you felt then and how you feel now. Be honest and open with yourself, even if it's complicated.

- **Be Specific:** Try to be as specific as possible when writing about your experiences. Describe the events, sensations, and emotions in detail. This can help you gain clarity and understanding of your feelings.
- **Focus on the Present:** While it's important to acknowledge past traumas, also focus on how they affect you in the present moment. Reflect on any lingering emotions or behaviors that may stem from childhood experiences.
- **Express Gratitude:** End each writing session on a positive note by expressing gratitude for something in your life. This can help shift your focus away from negative emotions and towards feelings of appreciation and resilience.

GENDER ROLES - BALANCING THE MASCULINE AND FEMININE

As briefly mentioned, Carl Jung introduced the concepts of the anima and the animus as fundamental aspects of his theory of the collective unconscious. These concepts explore the feminine and masculine dimensions present within each of us regardless of our biological sex and offer a fascinating framework for understanding how gender roles manifest in society.

Gaining clarity and insight into the complex interplay between the anima and animus, or masculine and feminine aspects of our psyches, also gives us deep insights about the Shadow. Sometimes, the stereotypes hold a grain of truth–macho men can be afraid of and suppress their feminine traits, such as vulnerability and so-called weakness. Ultra-girlie girls may conceal their more male characteristics, such as anger and ambition, behind a veil of femininity. It's vital to examine your own dark and light male and female aspects.

Anima and Animus Defined

Anima refers to the inner femininity present in males. Jung depicted the anima as a man's internal female counterpart or a personal muse, influencing his relationships with women and his feminine side. It represents emotional, nurturing, and intuitive qualities traditionally associated with femininity.

Animus represents the inner masculinity present in females. For Jung, the animus was the male figure within women's unconscious, influencing their thinking and social interactions. It encompasses qualities like logic, rationality, and strength, traditionally considered masculine traits.

> *"The anima and animus have tremendous influence because we leave the shadow to them."*
>
> — CARL JUNG

Manifestation in Gender Roles

Jung's concepts of anima and animus suggest that every person possesses both feminine and masculine qualities. This duality influences our behaviors, preferences, and the roles we assume in society. Here's how these aspects can manifest in gender roles.

Complementarity in Relationships: The anima and animus play a significant role in heterosexual relationships by fostering a psychological bond between men and women. Men might be drawn to women who embody the qualities of their anima, whereas women might seek men reflecting their animus traits. This attraction to complementary characteristics can influence societal expectations of gender roles in partnerships and families.

Balancing Gender Roles: People might express traits associated with their anima or animus in professional settings or their personal interests, challenging traditional gender roles. For example, a man might embrace nurturing roles traditionally ascribed to women, such as caregiving or education. In contrast, a woman might pursue careers in fields dominated by men, such as engineering or leadership positions, reflecting the influence of her animus.

Personal Development and Integration: Jung believed that acknowledging and integrating the qualities of both the anima and animus is essential for psychological growth and wholeness. This process, which he termed individuation, involves reconciling these masculine and feminine aspects within oneself, leading to a more balanced and fulfilled life. As we strive for this balance, we may challenge societal gender norms and roles, contributing to more fluid and inclusive understandings of gender.

Cultural and Social Influences: The expression of anima and animus can also be shaped by cultural norms and socialization. Societies that encourage rigid gender roles might suppress the expression of the anima in men and the animus in women, leading to psychological tension or imbalance. Conversely, more egalitarian societies might encourage a healthier integration of these aspects, promoting more diversity in gender expressions and roles.

Jung's work on the anima and animus offers a nuanced understanding of the masculine and feminine forces within each of us, highlighting how these archetypes influence personal behaviour and societal gender roles. By recognizing and integrating these inner dimensions, we can challenge traditional roles, encourage a re-evaluation of gender and advocate for a more inclusive society that values the full spectrum of human qualities beyond the constraints of conventional gender norms.

Shadow Chronicle – Tara's Encounter

"I was maybe seven years old when I realised something was wrong with me. All the boys played with Lego and Minecraft, but I wanted to dress my sister's Barbie and make clothes for them. By 13 , I'd acknowledged to myself, if not the rest of the world, that I was gay, but my family was religious, so I assiduously hid it away from them. I suppressed all my desires to be feminine and, for years, even convinced myself I was straight. I was quiet at school, but I loved reading and English. I read "The Outsiders" by S.E. Hinton, and I realised the warring gangs in the book were like warring factions within me. I can't say what prompted this realisation, but it came like lightning bolt. As soon as I finished school, I left home and went as far away as I could from my Mid-West, conservative family. I moved to New York and finally released all the suffocated and concealed aspects of myself. At first, I was just into cross-dressing and drag, but over time, I realised I was trans. I'm transitioning, and whilst it's hard and painful, I'm becoming who I feel I was meant to be. I stopped fighting myself, and I finally feel whole."

Do You Dump?

The Socratic Questions you're about to discover are designed to help you explore the concept of ***projection***—how we often project or dump our Shadow onto others, seeing in them that we cannot see in ourselves. To help you identify the Shadow Traits you dislike, loathe, distrust and even hate in others, here's a list of what we often consider unacceptable human traits.

> *"Projections change the world into the replica of one's unknown face."*
>
> — CARL JUNG

Consider this list (not exhaustive by any means) and see whether there are any that you can identify in yourself first, then launch into the Socratic Questions to uncover more valuable information about how you behave in relationships and some of the unconscious drivers that motivate who you are when you relate to others. This understanding is crucial in developing healthier and more authentic relationships.

Shadow Traits are often those aspects of ourselves that we might be uncomfortable acknowledging or that society typically views as unfavorable. However, it's important to remember that recognising and understanding these traits can be a powerful step towards personal growth and self-awareness.

Shadow Traits

- Destructive
- Greedy
- Intolerant
- Mistrustful
- Defensive
- Aggressive
- Perverse
- Prejudiced
- Malicious
- Sarcastic
- Cynical
- Melancholic
- Moody
- Unforgiving
- Disrespectful
- Lazy
- Vindictive
- Overcritical
- Perfectionistic
- Negative
- Inflexible
- Envious
- Overindulgent
- Apathetic
- Despairing
- Escapist
- Fatalistic
- Gossipy
- Hostile
- Hypersensitive
- Impulsive
- Ungrateful
- Cruel
- Materialistic
- Narcissistic
- Rude
- Prideful
- Lustful
- Gluttonous
- Wrathful
- Slothful
- Insecure

- Fearful
- Manipulative
- Deceitful
- Jealous
- Resentful
- Arrogant
- Impatient
- Dishonest
- Anal
- Stubborn
- Pessimistic
- Callous
- Controlling
- Indecisive
- Hypercritical
- Cowardly
- Selfish
- Irresponsible
- Insensitive
- Impulsive
- Narrow-minded
- Passive
- Overbearing
- Miserable
- Vicious
- Predatory
- Suspicious
- Pretentious
- Timid
- Bitter

These traits, when acknowledged and worked through, can lead to a deeper understanding of oneself and can be transformative in personal development. Shadow Work encourages us not to eliminate or shun these traits but to understand and integrate them in a balanced and healthy way.

25 SOCRATIC QUESTIONS TO REVEAL SHADOW PROJECTION

- What feelings do I often notice when I'm upset with someone else's behavior?
- Can I identify traits in others that I find intolerable, which might also apply to me?
- How might my adverse reactions to others be a reflection of my inner conflicts?
- When I criticize others, what am I often criticizing about myself?
- Are there specific qualities in others that I admire or envy? What might these reveal about my desires or lack?
- When I feel misunderstood by others, is it possible that I am not fully understanding or accepting some part of myself?
- How do my judgments of others align with my insecurities about myself?
- In what ways might my past experiences be coloring my perception of others' actions?
- When do I find myself assuming others' motives? How often might these assumptions be wrong?
- How can I differentiate between someone's character and my perception of their character?
- What are the patterns in the types of people I have conflicts with? What does this tell me about myself?
- How might my childhood experiences influence the traits I project onto others?
- Can I think of a time when my perception of someone changed significantly? What prompted this change?

- How do my emotional needs affect how I perceive others' actions and words?
- When I think someone is unfair, could it be a sign of how I treat myself or others?
- How might my mood affect how I interpret others' behaviors and comments?
- In what situations do I overreact, and what might this tell me about my hidden aspects?
- How could recognizing and understanding my Shadow aspects change my relationships?
- If I feel consistently victimized in relationships, what part of my Shadow might be at play?
- How does my communication style reveal my projections onto others?
- Are there certain emotions I am uncomfortable expressing, and do I criticize others for showing these emotions?
- What aspects of myself am I most defensive about, and how does this defense manifest in my relationships?
- Can I recall an instance where I attributed my feelings or motives to someone else? What was the outcome?
- How might the roles I play in my relationships serve to hide aspects of my Shadow?
- What steps can I take to ensure I am not allowing my Shadow to distort my view of others?

These questions are designed to help guide you towards a deeper understanding of how the unconscious parts of your psyche—which may be projected onto others—can affect your relationships.

I urge you to explore them in a Journal one by one. As I've said before, insights into the Shadow are not accomplished overnight. Give yourself time and as much self-love and self-compassion as you can muster up to look at this stuff.

SHADOWS CAST BY THE DISOWNED SELF

In relationships, the Shadow can manifest in various ways, affecting dynamics and interactions with others. Understanding and integrating these Shadow aspects are crucial for healthy relationships. Here are some ways the Shadow shows up in relationships, paired with insights from leading lights in psychology and specific strategies to address these challenges.

Projection

Manifestation: We often project our disowned qualities onto others, criticizing or admiring traits in them that belong to our own Shadow.

Quote: Carl Jung famously said, "Everything that irritates us about others can lead us to an understanding of ourselves."

Combat Strategy: Practice self-awareness and reflection. When you notice a strong negative or positive reaction to someone, ask yourself, "What part of me might be reflected in this reaction?" Engaging in journaling or therapy can aid in uncovering these projections.

Fear of Intimacy

Manifestation: The Shadow can cause us to fear true intimacy because getting close to someone might reveal what we've hidden from ourselves.

Quote: The famous Jungian analyst Marion Woodman observed, "Fear of the feminine leads to a barricading against personal intimacy."

Combat Strategy: Build trust in yourself and your worthiness of love. Engage in dialogues about vulnerabilities with trusted mentors or coaches or a therapist to gradually dismantle these fears.

Repetition of Past Hurts

Manifestation: Unresolved Shadow aspects can lead us to recreate situations that mirror past traumas or hurts unconsciously or hurts.

Quote: Robert A. Johnson suggests, "We're doomed to repeat history if we're not conscious of our shadow."

Combat Strategy: Recognize patterns in your relationships. Mindfulness and therapy, especially with a focus on Shadow Work, can help heal old wounds and change repetitive behaviors.

Power Struggles

Manifestation: The Shadow can lead to power struggles within relationships, where dominance and submission dynamics play out unconsciously.

Quote: Clarissa Pinkola Estes teaches us that "The struggle for power in a relationship is a dance of shadows."

Combat Strategy: Cultivate open communication and practice assertiveness. It's essential to express needs and boundaries clearly and listen to the other's perspective.

Jealousy and Envy

Manifestation: These emotions can often be Shadow expressions, revealing our insecurities and unfulfilled desires.

Quote: James Hillman believed that "Envy and jealousy stem from the shadowy parts of our psyche that we refuse to acknowledge fully."

Combat Strategy: Acknowledge and explore these feelings without judgment. Understanding what these emotions are signalling about your desires and self-esteem can help address the underlying issues.

DOING THE HARD YARDS - OWNING YOUR STUFF

You may be one of the rare creatures roaming this earth who has never hurt or upset another living soul. But if you're a mere mortal like the rest of us, you are likely to have left a wake from time to time as you did what every human does – make mistakes, mess up, hurt people, and, in so doing, harm yourself. Don't stress. There are ways to address the past and take ownership of your shit. Creating a script for such a difficult and profound conversation requires careful thought, sensitivity and empathy. This script aims to facilitate a respectful and sincere dialogue, acknowledging your shortcomings and their impact on others. Adjustments may be needed based on the specific relationship and context:

Setting the Tone

You: "Hey [Name], do you have a moment? I've been doing some reflecting, and there's something important I need to talk to you about. It's about me and some things I've come to realise about my actions in the past. I really value our relationship, and I believe this conversation is a step towards understanding and growth for me. Is now a good time?"

Acknowledgment and Taking Responsibility

You: "I've been thinking a lot about how I've acted in our relationship and others in the past. I've realised that sometimes my behavior was not okay, and I wasn't the best version of myself. I've been learning about the concept of the Shadow—the parts of ourselves we're not proud of or don't always recognise. I see now how my Shadow side has impacted you and our relationship negatively."

Specific Apologies

You: "I want to specifically apologise for [mention specific behaviors or instances]. I can see how my actions [describe the impact of your actions] might have hurt you or made things difficult. I'm truly sorry for the pain I've caused. My intention was never to hurt you, but I understand that intentions aren't enough, and the impact of my actions is what truly matters."

Expressing Personal Growth and Future Intentions

You: "Reflecting on this has been a humbling experience. I'm working on understanding and integrating these parts of myself to become more aware and responsible for how I show up in relationships. This includes [mention any therapy, reading, or self-reflection you are doing]. I'm committed to changing my behavior because I deeply care about you and our relationship."

Openness to Feedback

You: "I'm here to listen to how you feel, your thoughts, and any impact I might not be fully aware of. Your perspective is invaluable, and I want to understand your experience. Please feel free to share anything whenever you're ready. I'm committed to making things right and rebuilding trust, however long that may take."

Closing - Reaffirming Commitment to Change

You: "I know apologies are just the start, and it's my actions moving forward that will truly count. I'm dedicated to doing the work, both for myself and for the health of our relationship. Thank you for listening and giving me the space to share this with you. How would you like to move forward from here? And I want you to know that not continuing our relationship is OK, too."

Remember, the goal of this conversation is not just to apologize but also to demonstrate a genuine commitment to personal growth and healing. It's essential to be prepared for a range of responses, including the possibility that the other person may need time to process or not fully engage in the conversation. Respect their feelings and give them the space they need.

HEALING WOUNDS WITH LIGHT

Forgiveness is the balm that can soothe the deep cuts of the soul, allowing us to heal wounds that fester in the deep recesses of our Shadow. Its role in healing is as transformative as it is essential, particularly for those Shadow aspects rooted in trauma, hurt and resentment. Forgiveness is not about condoning harm or absolving others for their actions; it's about freeing yourself from the heavy burden of past pains. Forgiveness is ultimately a self-loving act.

The process of forgiving both oneself and others is a critical step on the path to healing. It begins with acknowledging the hurt without allowing it to define you. Forgive yourself for the times you might have reacted out of pain and for not knowing the full extent of your resilience. Forgive others, not because they necessarily deserve it, but because you deserve the peace forgiveness can bestow. Letting go is a declaration of self-respect and a commitment to moving forward.

To cultivate real and lasting forgiveness, there are several practices you can employ.

- Reflective journaling can be a powerful exercise where you express and then dismantle the hurt.
- Meditative practices focused on loving-kindness help to soften the heart towards oneself and others.
- Affirmations of forgiveness, repeated with intention, can reshape thought patterns from resentment to release.
- Sometimes, visualizing the person you wish to forgive (including yourself) and mentally offering forgiveness can also shift internal blockages.

The liberating power of forgiveness lies in its ability to unshackle us from the chains of the past. As we release these bonds, we open ourselves to wholeness and self-love that is both rich and thoroughly liberating. Through forgiveness, we allow light to penetrate the shadows, making room for growth, healing, and a future unburdened by the weight of past pain. Forgiveness, in its truest form, is an act of profound courage and one of the best forms of self-care on the journey to inner peace.

Here are ten specially crafted **Forgiveness Affirmations** to add, when needed, to your daily Shadow Work practice.

- I choose to forgive those who have hurt me and set myself free from holding onto bitterness.
- Forgiveness is a gift I give myself, and I willingly release the burden of resentment.
- I am capable of moving beyond my past hurts and embracing the present with an open heart.
- Each day, I allow forgiveness to heal my heart and mind, bringing peace and freedom.
- I acknowledge my pain, but I choose to forgive and grow stronger from my experiences.
- Forgiveness does not change the past, but it does enlarge the future. I choose a future of peace.
- I am releasing the power that my past has over me through forgiveness.
- By forgiving others, I reclaim my power and refuse to be defined by my past.
- I forgive myself for my mistakes and learn from them, knowing that self-forgiveness is the first step toward a brighter future.
- I embrace forgiveness as an act of compassion toward myself and others, knowing it frees us all.

BOUNDARY WORK - AN ESSENTIAL COMPONENT OF SHADOW WORK

Establishing balanced energetic boundaries is a vital component of maintaining emotional and spiritual well-being. These invisible barriers are our personal space guardians, preserving our energy and protecting us from being overly influenced by others' emotions and thoughts.

We've all heard the term psychic vampires. It's the feeling of being drained after seeing a friend who unloads their problems onto you or the actual physical discomfort of someone standing too close and invading your space. These are everyday and common signs that your energetic boundaries have been compromised. Just as a fence around a garden keeps out pests, energetic boundaries shield us from emotional overload and psychic debris.

Identifying when these boundaries have been crossed is the first step to reclaiming your space. You might feel irritable, anxious or tired—these emotional cues can reveal a need to examine which interactions are depleting you. It could be as subtle as someone negating your experiences as "gaslighting" or as overt as unwelcome physical contact. Becoming aware of these violations helps you take steps to enforce your boundaries.

Creating and maintaining boundaries involves self-awareness and assertiveness. Start by getting clear on your limits:

- What you are willing to accept from others and what you are not.
- Communicate these limits clearly and calmly. Use affirmative language such as, "I appreciate our discussions, but I need to focus on my work right now," or "I am not comfortable with this topic; let's talk about something else."
- Practice saying "No" without feeling guilty; it's a right, not a luxury.

In daily life, visualizing a warm, protective golden light shield around you can help maintain these boundaries energetically. Also, incorporate activities that reinforce your sense of self, such as meditation, spending time in nature, or any hobbies you enjoy and find fun and replenishing. Crucially, be careful about the company you keep. The friendships that you have and the people you surround yourself with play a huge role in how you feel and the influence they have on your life.

Setting boundaries as a form of self-care is super-powerful, especially within the context of Shadow Work and integration. As we work through our Shadow aspects, it's vital to protect our slightly vulnerable and emerging selves from energies that can hinder the process. A strong sense of boundaries allows us to interact with others from a place of compassion and safety without losing ourselves in their psychic baggage.

SELF-LOVE MINDFULNESS MEDITATION

OK, so you've been doing a lot of heavy lifting! Owning our Shadow in relationships is not for the faint-hearted; it takes courage and true grit!

Here is a guided self-love mindfulness meditation designed to foster self-compassion. This meditation draws from the principles of Mindfulness-Based Stress Reduction (MBSR) developed by Jon Kabat-Zinn and the work on self-compassion by Dr Kristin Neff, a pioneering researcher in the field of self-compassion and one of the founders of The Center for Mindful Self-Compassion

Self-Love Mindfulness Meditation

Step 1.

Move to a comfortable place to sit or lie down without interruptions. Close your eyes or lower your gaze, whichever feels more comfortable.

Step 2.

Take a deep breath in, feeling your lungs expand with air, and as you exhale, let go of any tension you are holding. With each breath, allow yourself to sink a little deeper into relaxation.

Step 3.

Now, bring your attention to your heart. Imagine a soft, warm light glowing there, radiating kindness and love. With each breath, this light grows brighter, filling you with peace and compassion.

As you continue to breathe, repeat these phrases silently to yourself:

"May I be happy."

"May I be healthy."

"May I be safe."

"May I live with ease."

Feel the meaning of each word, allowing the intentions to wash over you like a soothing wave. If your mind wanders, gently guide your attention back to these phrases.

Step 4.

Now, think of a moment when you were critical of yourself. Observe this memory without judgment, as if you are watching a cloud passing in the sky. Offer kindness to that part of you that was suffering. You might say to yourself:

"I am learning and growing every day."

"I forgive myself for my mistakes."

"I accept myself as I am."

Step 5.

Visualize extending compassion to that past version of yourself, as you would to a dear friend. Allow the warm light in your heart to envelop this memory, transforming it with understanding and love.

For the next few minutes, sit with this feeling of self-compassion, letting it fill every part of your being. If your mind wanders, return to the warmth in your heart and the compassionate phrases.

Step 6.

As we end this meditation, take a few deep breaths, bringing your awareness back to the present. Wiggle your fingers and toes, and when you're ready, open your eyes.

Note: Remember, this light of compassion is always within you, ready to offer warmth and love whenever you need it.

By integrating the Shadow through conscious work self-acceptance, and ultimately self-love, you can move from fragmented self-experience to a sense of wholeness. This is the essence of healing in Jungian therapy—acknowledging and bringing to light the parts of ourselves that have been hidden, thereby transforming our relationship with ourselves and, by extension, with others.

CHAPTER SIX

SHADOW MASTERY AND MANIFESTING

In the dimly lit corridors of our psyche lies the Shadow, that elusive and often misunderstood aspect of ourselves. It is the repository of all we deny, the characteristics we shun, and the impulses we fear. Yet, within this darkness, there exists a profound source of creativity, vitality, and untapped power.

This chapter delves into the intricate play between the Shadow and the art of manifesting our deepest desires. We'll unravel how the Shadow, with its hidden strengths and qualities, powerfully influences our goals, dreams, and ambitions.

Far from being a hindrance or a hurdle to jump over, the Shadow is the chalice that contains many of the raw materials of our potential greatness. By courageously confronting and integrating our Shadow, we unlock a wellspring of creativity and aliveness that propels us toward our aspirations. This process of reconciliation not only illuminates the path to achieving our ambitions but also enhances our connection to the authentic self. It invites a transformation that cultivates a sense of wholeness—where every facet of our being contributes to manifesting a life of purpose, joy, and fulfilment.

As we venture deeper into the velvety darkness of our hidden selves, we discover that embracing our Shadow is not just an act of healing; it is a powerful declaration of our intention to live fully, dynamically and unapologetically and in doing so, release our inner Oracle to do in a single lifetime what it was born to do—heal you and at the same time heal the earth.

Transformation is the very essence of Shadow Work. This chapter focuses on turning the potentially negative aspects of your Shadow into positive

strengths–strengths you can harness to master your darkness and use those traits to manifest your goals and dreams. After all, what are you here for other than to change your role from puppet to puppeteer?

You're going to visualise a future where you're whole. And from that place of wholeness, you're going to learn how to craft the life of your dreams using powerful manifesting tools. The writing prompts in this chapter will invite you to rewrite your story in a way that gives you power and agency, propelling you out of the role of victim into the exalted position of story-teller and hero. This exercise is not just about imagination; it's about recognizing the potential and strength within your Shadow.

Embracing your Shadow is not about eradicating it but transforming its energy into something constructive and life-affirming. By the end of this chapter, you'll see your Shadow not as an adversary but as a source of untapped potential and power.

REWRITING YOUR STORY - AN EXERCISE IN POWER

Even though it's something you repeat over and over, you've probably never properly tuned into the story you tell yourself about your life. This story is the cornerstone of all the limiting beliefs you harbor about yourself and the world that keep you stuck and stalled, fearful and frozen, lacklustre and lethargic. You may not have known this, but your inner dialogue about your past dramatically informs your expectations of your future. It can lay out before you a landscape of broken hopes, unfulfilled dreams and anticipated disappointment over what's in store for you.

When you repeat a sad story, it becomes a brainwashing mantra, a version of toxic self-hypnosis that, without some work, can be tricky to rewire.

But your story is also a rich storehouse of energy and possibility. When you engage with it, embrace it, and learn how to rewrite it, you unlock vast resources of self-confidence and self-love. Most importantly, you release yourself to enjoy the future you desire.

Now, it's time to write your unvarnished story–make sure it's unedited and unabridged; no one else is going to read this (unless you give permission to share it in a safe way). Give yourself the space to write about the highs and lows, the hurts and fears, the misdemeanours, mistakes and redemptions. Are you the hero or heroine of your story, or are you the villain, the fool or the victim?

Don't leave anything out. Include the turning points when you got bad news, lost someone, or failed terribly. Equally, record accurately the times you triumphed, succeeded against the odds, gave unconditionally, and loved passionately. Don't sugar-coat and dazzle with positivity—this is your opportunity to be real and honest with yourself.

Let's be honest; this is often a painful exercise. Being unconditionally frank with yourself takes guts and true grit. Most people don't want to shine a light on their dark side, and to do this exercise properly, so you get the genuine benefits from it (which I promise are huge when you do it with a whole heart), you need to get tough and get real.

This exercise may take more than one day to complete. Go through any old diaries, old photos and mementos to remind you of who you were. At the same time, it's also worthwhile to construct a vision board of who you want to be in your future and embellish it with pictures, affirmations and trinkets that inspire and delight you.

Writing your story like this is probably a one-in-a-lifetime thing. The reason is that it's such a paradigm shift, so pivotal, that the person you were before it is not the same person you'll be when you complete it. If you need the support of a professional helper–a coach, mentor, parent, trusted friend or therapist, don't be afraid to reach out for an ally in this process.

I'm suggesting other writing tasks in this Workbook, but for this exercise, create a timeline and use it as a roadmap from birth to 5 years old, then from 6 to 10 years old, 11 to 15 years old, going up in five-year increments until the present moment. On the timeline, mark the places where significant events took

place–everything from starting school to your first boyfriend or girlfriend, big family moments such as divorce or death of a loved one, first pet, finishing school and college, first job and so on. The timeline serves as an objective record of your life events.

Next, take your journal and begin by looking at the life events, especially anything that caused you trauma and write down your feelings next to the event. For example: "Started school and was bullied on the first day. Felt awful, afraid, rejected and helpless. That feeling of being a five-year-old and not being safe is still with me today".

Once you've gone through the critical events on the timeline, pull out all the core beliefs you've discovered about yourself and create a list to identify the thoughts you carry with you today. Going back to the five-year-old who was bullied—the core beliefs may be: "I'm helpless", "I'm worthless", "I'm powerless".

We humans tend to distort our past unintentionally. Our stories become exaggerated and dramatic as we attribute meaning to events with our creative imagination. Events from our childhood become reasons why we are not good enough. To a child, life is confusing, and the only way to make sense of it is to make it about themselves. When they see their mother stressed or their father angry, they believe it's their fault. These beliefs keep us anxious and feed our fears.

One of the keys to the power of this exercise is that you become conscious of the thoughts (mostly from childhood and early adolescence) you're still holding onto. The good news is that now you're an adult and have agency and choice, so you can rewrite the past and give it an entirely new spin.

Now you're ready for the fun part—the moment when you take control of your narrative. It's time to let go of your old story and start afresh. Writing your new story is about embracing your past, the trauma, and the negative self-talk and rewriting it from a magnificently empowered perspective.

This is how to start.

Let your imagination run wild and permit your mind to roam free. Sit down in a quiet space. Put on your favorite playlist and write your story from the perspective of a journalist writing a profile piece about a rock star, great artist, CEO, boss–whoever you want to be. And, by the way, you can also just envision yourself, but the version that doesn't have any pain and without any limits. Make sure you include all your positive traits and your quirks because they're the parts of yourself that are authentically you. There's no limit on what you write or how much. You might fill a book or just write a page–it's fine, whatever feels right in the moment.

It's time to apply a little self-discipline and stop telling the old story. You'll notice when you're triggered that you unconsciously revert to old self-talk habits. That's OK. When you see your mind drifting back to familiar tracts of thought, gently move it towards the new path, the one where you're in control of your own story.

The changes will take a little while to bed down, but you'll notice in just a matter of days that your awareness of those old stories has vastly improved. And when you see those moments, that's the point of power; it's when you get to change the narrative.

THE SHADOW AND YOUR GOALS AND ASPIRATIONS

Because so few of us tap into our Shadows, we often walk through our lives on autopilot. We rarely notice where our impulses spring from; we hardly ever deconstruct whether it's truly our will operating the system or our parent's, or society's will that is propelling us. The good news is that Shadow Work challenges our assumptions about ourselves, our histories and our futures and puts us in the driver's seat of our lives. Being a passenger in this ride called life, no longer becomes an option. Bad luck if you wanted to stay in a somnambulant state! Shadow Work wakes you up to the possibilities of life and gives you the license to drive.

One of the keys to mastering this work is to use our Shadow traits in positive ways.

Channel Anger Constructively

Anger often signals boundaries being crossed or unmet needs. Instead of suppressing it, use anger as a motivator to take action towards your goals. Let it fuel your ambition rather than destructiveness, directing this energy towards positive change.

Harness Ambition

Ambition, when motivated by insecurity, can be destructive. However, when aligned with one's true values and goals, it becomes a powerful force for achieving success. Use your ambition not for comparison or competition but as a drive to fulfil your potential.

Creative Expression

The Shadow often contains unexplored creativity. Engage in creative activities without judgment or expectation. This free expression can unlock innovative ideas and solutions, propelling you towards your dreams.

Transform Fear into Courage

Fear often resides in the Shadow, masking our deepest desires and potential. By facing these fears directly, we can transform them into courage. This act of bravery opens the path to pursuing our dreams with resilience and determination.

EXCAVATING YOUR VALUES

One of the first steps to manifesting the life you've always wanted is to get in touch with your values.

Your values are the principles, standards, or qualities you consider essential or desirable. These values guide your behaviour, influence decision-making, and shape priorities and interactions with others. They often reflect what you believe is critical in life, both morally and ethically, as well as in terms of personal goals or aspirations.

Some examples:

- **Honesty:** Being truthful and transparent in one's actions and words.
- **Integrity:** Adhering to moral and ethical principles and doing the right thing in all circumstances, even when no one is watching.

- **Respect:** Showing consideration and appreciation for others, their feelings, and their rights.
- **Compassion:** Showing empathy and kindness towards others and a desire to help those in need.
- **Responsibility:** Taking accountability for one's actions and being reliable.
- **Fairness:** Treating people equally, making judgments without discrimination, and ensuring justice.
- **Courage:** Facing challenges and fears head-on and standing up for what is right despite adversity.
- **Loyalty:** Being faithful and devoted to someone or something, showing steadfast allegiance.

Opening Up to Your Qualities

OK, so your qualities are most likely not hidden within the confines of your Shadow. Most often, your qualities or traits are the distinguishing characteristics or attributes that make up your personality–and you'll probably be pretty familiar with them. These can include aspects of behaviour, temperament, and emotional patterns that are consistent over time. Your qualities or traits define how you typically think, feel, and behave, influencing your interactions with others and your approach to various situations in life.

By no means an exhaustive list, but here are some examples:

- **Empathy:** The ability to understand and share the feelings of others.
- **Resilience:** The capacity to recover quickly from difficulties; mental and physical toughness and grit.
- **Curiosity:** A strong desire to learn or know something, leading to exploration and discovery.

- **Adaptability:** The ability to adjust to new conditions or environments.
- **Innovativeness:** The use of imagination or original ideas to create something; inventiveness.
- **Optimism:** Hopefulness and confidence about the future or the successful outcome of something.
- **Patience:** The capacity to accept or tolerate delay, trouble, or suffering without getting angry or upset.
- **Determination:** Firmness of purpose; the resolve to achieve a goal despite obstacles.
- **Integrity**: Adherence to strong moral and ethical principles.
- **Humility**: Having a modest view of one's importance and being open to learning from others.
- **Compassion**: A deep awareness of and sympathy for the suffering of others, combined with a desire to help.
- **Patience**: The ability to endure difficult situations without becoming angry or upset.
- **Courage**: The ability to confront fear, pain, danger, or adversity with bravery.
- **Gratitude:** The quality of being thankful and showing appreciation for kindness.
- **Honesty**: The quality of being truthful and transparent in actions and words.
- **Generosity**: The willingness to give more of something, such as time or resources, than is strictly necessary or expected.

Once you've done an inventory of your values and qualities, you'll have an outline or map of who you are and what's important to you. The next part is the exciting bit. Here's where you get to have fun. If your traits reveal that you are a compassionate and empathetic person, maybe you could consider a path in life that aligns your values with your personality traits? Perhaps you'd like to mentor troubled teens or start a fund for a women's refuge in your area. If you're super-money oriented maybe you'd like to make your first million before your 30th birthday. Your dreams and goals will become so much easier to achieve when you align your qualities with your values. Why? Because this is a formula for an inspired, happy and fulfilled life. There's an easy equation here:

QUALITIES + VALUES = PASSION & PURPOSE

Fuel to the Fire

So, now that you've figured out your values and qualities and how they contribute to your passion and purpose, here's the real secret sauce. When you bring all the hidden talents, abilities, suppressed desires, and unacknowledged gifts to the

table–you become incredibly powerful. The most powerful people know how to channel their rage, jealousy, invulnerability, fury, sexuality, wrath, hatred, prejudice and lust for power in ways that get them what they want. Don't get me wrong, it's not about unleashing all your negativity on others, it's about using those often-shunned emotions usually locked within the Shadow to create and manifest what you want. When we're afraid of who we are, all the ugliness inside us, that ugliness usually gets projected onto other people. What I am suggesting here is the opposite–when we consciously and conscientiously own our darkness, it becomes a tool we can use.

Don't be afraid of your dark feelings. Channel them into your passion and purpose in life.

> *"Usually, when people are sad, they don't do anything. They just cry over their condition. But when they get angry, they bring about a change."*
>
> — MALCOLM X

THE SHADOW AT WORK

In the work environment, the Shadow can manifest through behaviors and attitudes that reflect repressed emotions, desires, and vulnerabilities. This often surfaces in office politics, gossip, interpersonal dramas, bullying, harassment, and power games. These manifestations are not merely individual but can permeate the culture of a workplace, influencing dynamics and relationships in subtle or overt ways.

Many of us have been victims of office politics—reeling as we stand on the sidelines, watching with horror as individuals or groups manoeuvre to gain advantage or influence, frequently at the expense of others. This can reflect the Shadow's desire for power and recognition. Gossip and dramas similarly reveal the Shadow through the spreading of rumours or engaging in behaviours that stir conflict and division, often stemming from jealousy, insecurity, or a desire for attention.

Bullying and harassment are more direct manifestations of the Shadow, where individuals may project their insecurities and frustrations onto others, causing terrible harm. This behavior not only reflects the bully's internal struggles but also affects the victim's self-esteem and well-being. Power games involving manipulative tactics to control or demean others also highlight the Shadow's influence in creating toxic work environments.

Combating these Shadow manifestations requires a multifaceted approach–and no one will say this is easy! Calling out workplace Shadows can be a scary thing, especially if your livelihood depends on that job or role.

Here's what you can do.

Self-awareness and Reflection

Start by engaging in your own introspection, recognizing the parts of yourself that might be projected onto others. Mindfulness and self-reflection practices can facilitate this understanding.

Open Communication

Cultivating a culture of transparency and open dialogue can help address underlying tensions and conflicts. Encouraging employees and colleagues to voice concerns and experiences in a safe environment can lead to resolutions before issues escalate.

Professional Development

Training programs focusing on emotional intelligence, conflict resolution, and effective communication can equip employees with the skills to navigate and mitigate Shadow manifestations in the workplace.

Supportive Leadership

Leaders play a crucial role in setting the tone for workplace culture. By modelling inclusive and respectful behaviour, leaders can discourage toxic dynamics and promote a positive, collaborative environment.

Access to Resources

Providing access to counselling services or employee assistance programs (EAPs) can support o those affected by negative Shadow manifestations. EAPs provide confidential support for employees facing personal or professional challenges. This can include mental health counselling, legal assistance, financial planning services, and crisis intervention, supporting employees' overall well-being.

If you've been affected by workplace bullying or harassment, contact a counsellor, therapist or legal practitioner who has experience in the area of workplace health and safety.

Addressing the Shadow in the work environment is crucial for a healthy, productive, and supportive workplace culture. By recognizing and addressing these unconscious aspects of ourselves and others, individuals and organizations can create a more positive and inclusive work environment.

MANIFESTING THE LIFE YOU WANT - THE SMART WAY

Goal setting is one of the most powerful tools to have your self-love back pocket. Why? Setting goals and achieving them makes you feel like a warrior. The Shadow loves to convince us that life is against us and we swim against the tide. Setting goals and achieving them puts the Shadow on notice that we're no longer listening to the negative voices in our heads, and we're going for it–no matter what!

Achieving goals provides clear evidence that you're more powerful than you imagined. Commit to yourself every day and stay strong and focused. Nothing is impossible when you're clear and intentional about what you want out of life and you go wholeheartedly after it. Ask any successful person, and they'll tell you setting goals is how they got from A to B. Here's a leaf out of the success handbook–with SMART goals nothing can hold you back–not even your Shadow!

Set SMART (Specific, Measurable, Achievable, Relevant, Timebound) goals! This useful acronym helps you create the life you want with clarity, direction and motivation.

Here's how to do it:

Step 1.

Identify Your Goal

Begin by clearly defining your goal. What do you want to achieve? The more precise, the better.

Step 2.

Make It Specific (S)

Ask yourself: What exactly do I want to accomplish? Be as specific as possible. Instead of a vague goal like "get in shape," a specific goal might be "lose 10 pounds in three months."

Step 3.

Make It Measurable (M)

Determine how you'll measure your progress and success. What indicators will show you're moving in the right direction? In our example, measuring weight loss in pounds is a precise measure.

Step 4.

Make It Achievable (A)

Consider whether your goal is realistic and attainable. Is it within your capabilities and resources? Make sure it's challenging, yet possible. For instance, losing 10 pounds in three months may be realistic for some but not for others, so adjust as needed and be kind to yourself in the process.

Step 5.

Make It Relevant (R)

Ask yourself why this goal matters to you. How does it align with your values and long-term objectives? Ensure your goal is relevant and meaningful in your life.

Step 6.

Make It Time-Bound (T)

Set a specific timeframe for achieving your goal. Without a deadline, there's no sense of urgency. In our example, "three months" provides a clear timeframe.

Step 7.

Write It Down

Once you've completed the SMART criteria for your goal, write it down in a clear and concise statement. For example: "I will lose 10 pounds in three months by following a healthy diet, exercising regularly, and checking in with achievements every week." Remain accountable to yourself.

Step 8.

Create an Action Plan

Break down your SMART goal into smaller, actionable steps. What must you do each week or month to progress toward your goal? Develop a plan that includes these steps.

Step 9.

Monitor and Adjust

Regularly review your progress. Are you on track to meet your goal within the specified timeframe? If not, adjust your action plan as needed to stay on course.

Step 10.

Celebrate Achievements

Celebrate your successes along the way. Recognize and reward yourself when you achieve milestones or reach your goal. For example, if you want to lose weight, reward yourself with some new gym gear and think of the money you will save not binging on junk food. These positive reinforcements can help keep you motivated.

Setting SMART goals is a dynamic process. As you make progress, you'll gain new insights, and if you stay flexible and committed, you'll be well on your way to achieving your objectives!

SECRET MANIFESTING TOOLS

Manifesting, the practice of bringing something tangible into your life through attraction and belief, is often discussed in the context of personal development and spirituality. Here are ten powerful manifesting techniques that you can use to focus your intentions and achieve your goals. Use them often, and you'll be able to brush aside any whispers from the dark side that tell you don't deserve to have everything you want. Practice makes perfect.

Affirmations

Use these positive, present-tense statements and repeat them to yourself to boost your belief in your ability to achieve your goals. For example, saying "I am capable and deserving of success" daily reinforces a positive mindset and self-belief. Or "I attract everything I need and can create the future I desire".

Visualization

Dive into the practice of creating a mental image of your desired outcome. This involves vividly imagining achieving your goals, engaging all your senses to enhance the emotional impact and making the vision as accurate as possible.

Vision Boards

Make a physical or digital collage of images, quotes, and symbols representing your goals and dreams. Vision boards serve as a visual reminder of your aspirations, helping to focus your intentions and maintain motivation.

Scripting

Write down your desires in story form as if they have already happened. This technique involves detailing your dream life in the present tense, which can help solidify your desires and the emotions associated with achieving them. This is a powerful way to release your inner Oracle and learn to trust its wisdom and insights.

Gratitude Practice

Keeping a gratitude journal and regularly acknowledging things you are thankful for can shift your focus from what you lack to what you have. This positive mindset can attract more positivity into your life. It's also powerful to practice being grateful for your Shadow—this acceptance of who you are helps to integrate the light and dark aspects of the psyche, moving you another step towards individuation.

Affirmation Cards

Create cards with positive affirmations or inspiring quotes on them. Keeping them with you and reading them throughout the day can help keep your vibration high and your focus on your goals.

Letter to the Universe

Write a letter to the universe detailing your wishes and intentions as if you're having a conversation with a higher power. This can be a powerful way of letting go and trusting that your desires will come to fruition.

Acting "As If"

Behave "as if" you have already achieved your goal–this can help bring it into reality. This might include making decisions or taking actions that align with the future you desire, thereby aligning your current energy with that of your desired outcome.

Positive Environment

Surround yourself with positive people and environments that reflect the life you want to lead. This could involve joining groups with similar goals, creating a workspace that inspires you, or any action that immerses you in the energy of your desired outcome.

These manifesting techniques can be powerful tools in your personal development toolkit. However, it's important to remember that manifestation works best when combined with action and effort toward your goals. No matter what, these techniques will help you bring your Shadow out of the darkness and into the light—releasing a surge of self-love and acceptance.

THE JEWEL IN THE SHADOW WORK CROWN - CREATING YOUR OWN ORACLE DECK

Creating a personal Oracle Deck can be a deeply personal and transformative process, especially when it is intended for Shadow Work. Your creative impulses, often locked in the Shadow's vault, can be used as a powerful way to unleash your sacred and secret self.

Imagine creating your own divination deck for guidance. Well, you're about to learn how to do just that! You won't find *this revolutionary and unique creative exercise anywhere else*–I've created it expressly for you Shadow Workers with an eye for creativity and longing for guidance.

Here's a step-by-step guide to how to create and use your own Oracle Deck.

Designing Your Oracle Deck

Define Your Intentions: Before you begin, define what you want to achieve with your Oracle Deck. Since this deck is for Shadow Work, focus on themes that will help you explore and integrate the hidden parts of your psyche.

Choose a Structure: Decide on the number of cards and whether they will have a fixed structure or free-form. Some oracle decks may have a set number of cards with defined meanings, like a tarot deck, while others may be more fluid.

Create the Card Meanings: Write down the aspects of Shadow Work you want to address. This could be emotions, experiences, or archetypes. Each card will represent one of these elements.

- Hint: You could use power words or mantras and design a card around each word using images you love that relate to that word. For example, maybe you want to choose the word "Balance" and decide an image of a set of scales could accompany it.

Draft a Guidebook: Consider writing a companion guidebook that explains each card's significance and suggests ways to interpret them during a reading.

Selecting Imagery and Symbols

Personal Symbols: Select symbols and imagery that resonate with your journey. These should evoke a strong emotional or intuitive response from you.

Diverse Sources: Look for inspiration in various cultures, spiritual traditions, and personal experiences. Ensure that the imagery is respectful of its origins and relevant to the card 's meanings.

Visual Consistency: While the imagery should be varied, there should also be a unifying visual theme that ties the deck together, such as a color scheme or art style.

Artistic Creation: Create the artwork for your cards. You can draw, paint, use digital art, or even collage. The medium should be something you are comfortable with, and that reflects the deck's intention.

Using the Oracle Deck

Create a Ritual: Define a personal ritual for using your deck. This could involve lighting candles, meditating, or saying an intention or mantra aloud.

Ask Open-Ended Questions: When using the deck, focus on open-ended questions rather than yes/no questions. This invites deeper insight and reflection.

Draw Cards Intuitively: Shuffle the deck and draw cards at random or by feeling out which card(s) you are drawn to.

Reflect on the Imagery: Spend time looking at the imagery and symbols of the cards drawn and reflect on how they relate to your Shadow Work and the question you posed.

Integrating Oracle Readings into Shadow Work

Regular Readings: Incorporate regular Oracle readings into your Shadow Work practice. This could be daily, weekly, or any interval that feels right for you.

Journaling: After each reading, journal your thoughts, feelings, and any insights that arise. Note how the cards' messages may apply to your unconscious patterns or behaviors.

Action Steps: Use the insights from your readings to determine action steps. This could involve further self-reflection, therapy sessions, or creative expression.

Review and Reflect: Periodically review past readings and journal entries to see how your understanding and integration of your Shadow aspects have evolved.

This incredibly personal Oracle Deck, that you've designed and made is a powerful tool for introspection and growth. It doesn't need to conform to any standard other than what is meaningful to you on your passage to self-discovery. Revel in the pleasure and power of manifesting something only YOU can create. This special Shadow Work exercise is designed to help you become your own Oracle. Once you become adept at reading the messages that flow directly from your unconscious or higher self, you'll unlock a flood of intuitions and power.

Get ready to go beyond the realm of the ordinary as an initiate in the mysteries of the extraordinary.

CHAPTER SEVEN

BECOMING WHOLE - INTEGRATING THE SHADOW

In the profound journey of self-discovery, there lies a terrain often shrouded in mystery and, sometimes, apprehension—the realm of our Shadow. As you stand at the threshold of complete transformation, I invite you to step boldly and unflinchingly forward as you cross the bridge (never to return to that unenlightened shore again) to a more profound, authentic self.

Imagine the Shadow as not merely a repository of fears, faults, and vulnerabilities but as a sacred storehouse of untapped strength, creativity, and insight. It hints at our unacknowledged power and urges us to express the wild longings of our deepest desires. By venturing into this inner landscape, we confront not a foe but a friend in disguise, one who holds the keys to our fullest potential.

This chapter is a call to wholeness—it began many pages ago with a quest inward to explore the uncharted chambers that ordinarily reside outside our conscious knowledge, but now beckon beyond to the world outside ourselves where we may express our full selves.

Here's a message to heed—an Oracle to follow. If you take up this invitation to merge with the darkness, not to overcome it but to understand it and to integrate it, you will illuminate your entire being with the light of awareness and self-love.

As we travel through these pages together, let's hold space for every aspect of ourselves, embracing the Light and the Shadow with equal reverence. For it is in the marriage of these two forces that we find wholeness. It is here, in the heart of our willingness to see and be seen, that transformation occurs. We are not here to banish the Shadow but to weave it into the vibrant tapestry of our being, making us more complete, more resilient, and more authentically ourselves.

If you're this far into the book it's clear you have courage and grit. As I said at the beginning of this book Shadow Work is not for the lily-livered, shrinking violets of the world–this path is for warriors and wild ones, shamans, healers, dreamers, sword and dagger-wielders and the walkers on the path less travelled. Don't step onto this road if you're afraid of the gore of your old self, laid to waste and left to return to dust.

Becoming an Oracle, being integrated enough in yourself to hear the messages carried up from the unconscious to the conscious mind, has generally been reserved for those initiated into the mysteries of life. This often involved sacred rituals, carried on in secret ceremonies and demanded some sacrifice on the part of the initiate.

Sacred initiation rites appear across various cultures and spiritual traditions, including those of shamans, Witches, Druids, and indigenous peoples and serve as profound markers of transition, marking the passage of an individual from one state of being to another, often from a novice to a practitioner or from a practitioner to a master. These ceremonies can vary widely in their specifics, but they share common themes of transformation, connection to the spiritual realm, and the transmission of knowledge and power.

TRANSITIONING FROM THE ORDINARY INTO THE SACRED

We've borrowed from some of the most ancient traditions from around the world to help you transition from your old self to your new self–as a visionary, dreamer, seer, seeker, dreamer, modern shaman and Oracle.

Vision Quests or Spiritual Journeys

The initiate may undergo a solitary journey into the wilderness to seek visions or direct encounters with spirits or ancestors. This experience is central to receiving one's calling or spiritual powers.

Trial by Ordeal

In some traditions, the initiate may experience a form of physical trials, such as endurance of extreme temperatures, fasting, or isolation. Such trials are meant to test the spirit and resolve of the initiate, often believed to facilitate death-rebirth experiences crucial for a shaman's work.

Direct Transmission

In some cultures, specific knowledge, rituals, or powers are transmitted directly from a seasoned shaman to the initiate, often involving sacred rituals, the use of entheogens (psychoactive substances), and the passing of symbols of power like drums or other ritual objects.

Ceremonial Rituals

These might involve casting a circle, calling the elements, and invoking deity or deities, marking the formal entry into the group or circle.

Oath Taking

The initiate often takes vows of secrecy, loyalty, and commitment to the path. This may involve swearing on a sacred book or charter or an object or image imbued with special powers or symbolism.

Symbolic Death and Rebirth

Symbolizing the shedding of the old self and the birth of the new practitioner, these rituals mimic the cyclical nature of death and rebirth central to many sacred traditions.

Connection with Nature

Initiates often perform rituals in natural settings, such as forests, groves, or near bodies of water, to symbolize and facilitate a deep connection with the Earth.

Passage through Symbolic Gateways

Reflecting the transition from one state of being to another, initiates may pass through archways or doorways made of branches or stones, signifying entry into a new realm of knowledge and responsibility.

Mentorship and Learning

The path of an initiate into a mystery or religious school can involve years of learning about nature, the spiritual realm, and the lore of their tradition. It can involve study and questing and often includes becoming “apprenticed” to a master or mentor. Initiation might mark the beginning of this journey or the acceptance of the initiate into a new level of mastery.

Across all these traditions, initiation rites are profoundly transformative processes, meant not only to confer knowledge and power but also to integrate the novice more deeply into their community and the unseen world. These rites are tailored to the spiritual understanding and needs of the culture or tradition from which they arise, serving as a profound testament to the human connection with the divine, the natural world, and the community.

THE SUPREME TRANSFORMATION - FROM LEAD TO GOLD AND FROM THE ORDINARY SELF INTO THE SACRED ORACLE

This mystical initiation ritual, inspired by Carl Jung's alchemical concepts, is designed to transform you from your old self into a new, powerful mystic—and Oracle.

Jung saw alchemy as a symbolic process of inner transformation, with parallels to individuation—the journey towards wholeness and self-realization. Here, we've woven elements of alchemical symbolism and Jungian psychology into a ritual that guides you, the novice, towards mastery and mystical transformation.

Preparation

1. **Purification:** The initiate undergoes a period of purification to cleanse the mind, body, and spirit. This may involve fasting, meditation, and ceremonial cleansing baths, symbolizing the shedding of old, impure aspects of the self.
2. **Preparation of Sacred Space:** A sacred space is created, adorned with symbols representing the elements (earth, air, fire, water), the four cardinal directions, and celestial bodies. This space serves as a container for the transformative energies of the ritual.
3. **Invocation of Archetypes:** Archetypal figures such as the Wise Sage, the Mystic, and the Oracle are invoked, calling upon their wisdom and guidance to assist in the initiation process.

Ritual Phases

1. Nigredo (Blackening)

- The initiate confronts their Shadow self—the hidden, unconscious aspects of their psyche. This phase may involve guided introspection, journaling, and facing fears and unresolved traumas.

> *"Until you make the unconscious conscious, it will direct your life and you will call it fate."*
>
> — CARL JUNG

2. Albedo (Whitening)

- The initiate seeks purification and illumination. Through meditation, visualization, and contemplation, they strive to integrate their Shadow aspects with their conscious awareness, bringing light to the darkness.

> *"The meeting of two personalities is like the contact of two chemical substances: if there is any reaction, both are transformed."*
>
> — CARL JUNG

3. Citrinitas (Yellowing)

- The initiate experiences a heightened state of awareness and insight. Through symbolic acts such as receiving blessings from the ritual facilitators and communing with nature, they connect with the divine spark within themselves. If you are initiating yourself, you can use active imagination in this process and 'hear' and 'see' the facilitators in your mind's eye.

> *"Your vision will become clear only when you can look into your own heart. Who looks outside, dreams; who looks inside, awakes."*
>
> — CARL JUNG

4. Rubedo (Reddening)

- The culmination of the ritual is when the initiate experiences a symbolic death and rebirth. Through a guided visualization or enactment of a death-rebirth journey, they transcend their former self and emerge as Master of Oracles, ready to receive and transmit divine messages.

> *"There is no coming to consciousness without pain. People will do anything, no matter how absurd, in order to avoid facing their own soul. One does not become enlightened by imagining figures of light, but by making the darkness conscious."*
>
> — CARL JUNG

Conclusion of The Ritual

1. **Integration:** The initiate is welcomed into the community of masters and Oracles, symbolizing their integration of the sacred teachings and their readiness to fulfil their role as a conduit for divine wisdom.
2. **Celebration:** The ritual concludes with a celebratory feast and communal sharing of insights and visions. The initiate is honored for their courage and commitment to the path of transformation.

By blending Jungian psychology with alchemical symbolism, this initiation ritual aims to guide you, the novice, towards mastery and your oracular abilities, helping you unlock the hidden depths of your psyche and connect with the transcendent realms of the collective unconscious.

ACCEPTING DUALITY

We are not one thing or the other; we are all things at all times. One of the misconceptions of Shadow Work is that we're meant to banish the bad, the darkness, in favour of the light and goodness. This is incorrect. One is not better than the other. The path is, as they say in Buddhism, the Middle Way. It's a tightrope walk between the opposing forces within us.

The concept of duality is a central theme across many ancient philosophies and religions, often representing the interplay between light and dark, good and evil, or the conscious and unconscious. Jungian psychology, deeply rooted in similar mythological and religious concepts, offers a profound understanding of this interplay. Analyst Marion Woodman says, “There is no light without shadow and no psychic wholeness without imperfection.”

In Christianity, duality is depicted through the narrative of sin and redemption, a complex relationship between humanity's inherent sinful nature and the potential for salvation through grace. This tension invites believers to seek a path of humility and forgiveness, acknowledging their Shadows while striving for the light of Christ-like love and virtue.

Judaism addresses duality through the concept of yetzer hara (the evil inclination) and yetzer hatov (the good inclination). The Talmud teaches that both inclinations are necessary—the yetzer hara is not just an adversary but a force that, if harnessed correctly, can drive one’s ambition and adherence to God’s commandments.

In Buddhism, the duality of samsara (the cycle of rebirth and suffering) and nirvana (liberation from samsara) represents the journey from ignorance to enlightenment. Through mindfulness and meditation, one acknowledges the presence of desire and aversion, the Light and Shadow of the mind, leading to a balanced path of the Middle Way.

Hinduism portrays duality through a vast pantheon of deities representing various aspects of life and the cosmos, including light and dark forces. Practices like yoga and meditation in Hinduism are paths to experience the unity of atman (self) with Brahman (the ultimate reality), transcending duality.

Walking the path between the dark and light, as these traditions teach, is about embracing the full spectrum of existence. It’s a journey that requires confronting one’s own darkness with compassion and understanding. The Bhagavad Gita states,

"When a person responds to the joys and sorrows of others as if they were his own, he has attained the highest state of spiritual union."

One thing that is important to understand is the flow between Shadow and Light for the entire span of our earthly existence. We do not stand still once we have embraced the Shadow, we remain in a dynamic and active communication between the two opposing forces of our souls throughout our natural lives, which is continued into eternity. My brilliant Jungian analyst calls it a "conversation", where we learn to dialogue between these two aspects of ourselves so we stay whole, even while we are changing and in flux.

Do you feel different? Are you sensing the immense power at your fingertips? You're about to learn what to do with this newfound sense of power and agency and how to channel it for good—your good and the good of the planet.

Shadow Chronicle – Siddhartha's Path to Enlightenment

In a time out of mind in ancient India, beneath a canopy of starlit skies and the whispering of sacred rivers, a prince was born who became the hero of a tale as timeless as eternity itself. This is the story of Siddhartha, whose journey traversed the realms of desire, wisdom, and, ultimately, enlightenment.

As a young prince, born into luxury, Siddhartha roamed happily within the opulent walls of his father's palace, shielded from the sorrows that dwelt beyond its gilded gates. But as time went on the prince became bored with his privileged life and a yearning stirred within him—a yearning to unravel the mysteries of existence and to seek the secrets of the universe that seemingly eluded mortal grasp.

One night, compelled by an inner call, Siddhartha embarked on a pilgrimage, forsaking the comforts of the palace and all he'd known. He travelled the dusty roads and dirty backstreets where peasants scratched out a meagre existence as well as the verdant paths and sun-drenched meadows of his country. Along the way, he met the myriad faces of human suffering—the aged, the infirm and the lost as well as all the evils of the world—the greed, the envy, the cruelty and the despicable. The people's pain, burdens and lamentations echoed in the depths of his being, striking a chord of compassion he'd never heard before.

Siddhartha renounced his privilege and embraced the life of an ascetic, seeking solace in the quiet dark of the forest. For years he wandered alone, his spirit adrift on the currents of existence, his mind focused only on eternity. During this time, he mastered the disciplines of meditation and austerity—yet the truth he sought remained veiled, just a distant image flickering at the outer reaches of his consciousness.

One morning, as he rested under the shade of a generous Bodhi tree, Siddhartha vowed to part the veils that shrouded reality. With deep resolve, he delved into the depths of his own being, confronting the shadows that toyed with him, preventing his eyes from seeing the light of truth. Temptations assailed him, doubts besieged him—but he remained steadfast in his quest for enlightenment.

And then, in a moment that transcended the boundaries of time and space, illumination dawned on Siddhartha's newly awakened mind. Finally, he understood the interconnectedness of everything, the impermanence that weaves the fabric of existence and he understood that the end of suffering lies within the grasp of every human being.

At this moment all was transformed. Siddhartha, the seeker, became the Buddha, the awakened one, radiating the light of wisdom and compassion to all sentient beings. His teachings, like notes of a seductive tune borne upon the winds of time, continue to inspire seekers across the ages, beckoning them to tread the path of enlightenment and discover the boundless freedom that resides within.

CHAPTER EIGHT

THE BIG REVEAL - UNVEILING YOUR WHOLE AND INTEGRATED SACRED SELF TO THE WORLD

So, take a deep breath, Dear Shadow Worker, you are no longer the seeker; you have found yourself—your whole and sacred self. You have bound the Light and Dark sides of yourself together in a beautiful marriage of opposites. Like any union, there is tension at times, but balancing those opposing forces is part of your work as a Shadow Master.

And dare you ask....

Who are you now?

If I may be so bold, I will answer for you. You are the Oracle. You have emerged from the darkness, bearing a torch for all to see. The light is the wisdom you can convey in the form of sacred and mystical transmissions, intuitions, messages, dreams, insights, ruminations, advice, and whisperings from the world beyond the stars, where only mystics may see because they have pierced the veil of ignorance and have entered the world of the initiated.

Step forward with an open heart and a curious mind. The journey to integrating your Shadow and emerging transformed into the Oracle is the most noble and empowering quest you will ever undertake. It promises not just self-discovery but self-recovery and the joy of uncovering the boundless treasure within that has awaited your recognition all along.

Let us begin on a new adventure, one in which you are free to express your most luminous and undeniable entirety.

A unified person, one who has undergone the *individuation process* according to Jungian principles, possesses a profound capacity to contribute to collective healing. This individuated person embodies the integration of their dark and light aspects, achieving a harmonious balance that transcends polarities. Through their journey of self-discovery and inner alchemy, they have embraced the full spectrum of human experience, including the depths of their Shadow and the heights of their potential.

By reconciling their inner conflicts and accepting the totality of their being, the unified soul becomes a light of authenticity and wholeness in a fragmented world. They no longer project their unconscious fears and desires onto others—but instead hold space for the complexities of human existence with compassion and understanding. In their presence, others may find comfort and the inspiration to embark on their own paths of self-discovery and transformation.

The unified individual's contribution to collective healing is multifaceted. Firstly, their very existence serves as a reminder that healing is possible—that reconciliation and integration are attainable for anyone willing to embark on the journey of self-exploration. Secondly, as an Oracle, they may offer guidance and support to those who are navigating the tumultuous terrain of their own psyches, illuminating the path towards inner peace and fulfilment. Through their words and actions, they inspire others to confront their Shadows, embrace their authenticity, and cultivate empathy and compassion towards themselves and others.

The unified individual may act as a catalyst for societal change too, challenging oppressive systems and promoting inclusivity, equity, and justice. Their deepened understanding of human nature allows them to navigate complex social dynamics with wisdom and discernment, creating the right conditions for dialogue and collaboration towards collective healing and transformation.

In essence, the unified person's contribution to collective healing stems from their embodiment of wholeness and their commitment to authenticity, empathy, and social justice. They are not only agents of personal transformation but also catalysts for societal evolution, guiding humanity towards a more compassionate, inclusive, and harmonious future.

THE PROFOUND LEGACY AND IMPACT OF SHADOW WORK

Teaching Shadow Work

By openly sharing their own journey of Shadow integration, the unified individual can inspire others to embark on a similar path of self-discovery and inner healing. Through workshops, lectures, and written materials, they can provide tools and techniques for confronting and integrating the Shadow, empowering individuals to embrace their wholeness.

Guiding Organizational Transformation

In organizational settings, the unified individual can act as a catalyst for cultural change by fostering environments that encourage authenticity, vulnerability, and psychological safety. By facilitating workshops on Shadow dynamics, conflict resolution, and compassionate leadership, they can help organizations address systemic issues and cultivate healthier dynamics among team members.

Healing Relationships

Through their intuitive insights and empathetic understanding, the unified person can guide and support individuals and couples navigating relational challenges. By serving as a mediator, counsellor, or coach, they can facilitate deeper communication, mutual understanding and reconciliation, promoting healthier and more balanced relationships.

Inspiring Creative Expression

The unified soul's ability to tap into the collective unconscious and access symbolic wisdom as an Oracle can inspire artists, writers, and creatives to channel their innermost truths into their work. By encouraging creative expression as a tool for self-discovery and transformation, they can catalyze cultural shifts and spark collective dialogue around important social and spiritual themes.

Empowering Leadership

As mentors and coaches, unified people can empower emerging leaders to lead with authenticity, integrity, and compassion. By offering guidance on navigating power dynamics, ethical decision-making, and inclusive leadership practices, they can cultivate a new generation of conscious leaders who prioritize the well-being of their teams and communities.

Catalyzing Environmental Stewardship

Through their deep connection to the natural world and their recognition of humanity's interconnectedness with all life, unified individuals can advocate for environmental conservation and sustainability. By conveying messages of ecological wisdom and planetary interconnectedness, they can inspire people and organizations to adopt practices that honor and protect the Earth for future generations.

Facilitating Collective Rituals and Ceremonies

Unified individuals can organize and facilitate collective rituals and ceremonies that honor life transitions, seasonal cycles, and collective milestones. Drawing on their intuitive gifts and symbolic insights, unified souls can create transformative experiences that engender a sense of belonging, connection, and purpose within communities.

Writing and Sharing Wisdom

Through books, articles, blogs, and social media, unified souls can share their insights, teachings, and transmissions of wisdom with a global audience. By harnessing the power of storytelling and metaphor, they can convey timeless truths in accessible and relatable ways, reaching individuals across diverse backgrounds and cultures.

Advocating for Social Justice

Unified individuals can leverage their platform and influence to advocate for social justice, equity, and human rights. By speaking out against oppression, inequality, and injustice, they can amplify marginalized voices, mobilize collective action, and contribute to systemic change that uplifts and empowers all communities.

Modelling Authenticity and Integrity

Ultimately, the most potent legacy of a unified individual lies in the way they embody authenticity, integrity and compassion in their everyday actions and interactions. By modelling courage, vulnerability, and humility they set a powerful example for future generations, inviting others to embrace their own unique journey of growth, healing, and self-realization.

THE DIFFERENCE BETWEEN THE SHADOW AND THE ORACLE

Dr Robert A. Johnson, one of the world's experts on Jung, believed that at the very center of our being is a holy (or whole) place—the place where the ego and the Shadow come together and balance each other. The unification of these two opposing forces, he believed, is the true purpose of life.

The Shadow and the Oracle represent different voices and energies within us. The Shadow is the voice of the dark, disowned self, while the Oracle is the voice that speaks from our higher self—the holy part of ourselves. The Oracle is not the ego either. The ego relates to our conscious self and our personality. The Oracle bypasses both the Shadow and the ego to transmit messages that are much more subtle and sublime than anything that may issue from either the ego/conscious mind or the obscured, disowned self.

But here's the *great paradox*—we can't hear or see the messages clearly from the Oracle unless we have crossed the dark threshold of the Shadow. Once we are fully initiated into Shadow Work we can become true messengers of light. Without undertaking this journey, we may hear the murmurings of the Oracle but we cannot fully tune into their meanings or fully comprehend their wisdom.

Shadow Work forms a bridge between the ego and the Shadow and it is through this union, that our inner Oracle may be permitted to sing its full-throated song to all who will listen.

This is where the magic of Shadow Work comes into its own. When you can hear and see the transmissions with true clarity, you are an initiated one—individuated, en-lightened, wise and aware. Sacred and secret work that only *you* can master.

YOU - AS THE ORACLE STEPPING FORWARD AND OWNING YOUR POWER

As you take your first tentative steps into the world as a unified person, an *individuated human*, you will naturally feel a little scared. Don't be concerned; that is the echo of the Shadow rattling its chains to frighten you back to fragmentation. Fragmentation is a safe place. Nothing is really demanded of you while you're fragmented into dark and light; while conversely, being individuated, whole and unified demands something else. Right?

You may be a shy person who only wants to work on the self in the privacy of your own man or woman cave. That's fine. But something does happen when you become unified—suddenly, you feel an urgency to heal others, as well as yourself.

And let me clear something up: working on yourself this way certainly uplifts and changes the world around you. Your world and your relationships cannot help but be transformed by this mystical and sacred work.

You do not have to shout your wisdom from the rooftops or start a movement. All you have to do is acknowledge that once you are unified, you are not the same person anymore.

Indeed, individuated souls often do want to teach. And you find them amongst the wisest of our communities. Think of people like Malala Yousafzai, Martin Luther King, Albert Einstein, Eleanor Roosevelt and Greta Thunberg, who all wanted to change the world for the better. Perhaps they were adherents to some particular spiritual ideology, or maybe their path to greatness involved integrating their dark and light sides—we don't know for sure, but we do know that many great teachers are unified.

Without a particular path to individuation, the way can be fraught with perils, most notably, the fascination with power. It's a pitfall to be aware of. But having a path and a clear way forward gives you a structure so that if you do stumble, or even fall, there are guardrails to protect you.

Being an Oracle is not for the fainthearted. Being the receptacle of wisdom and allowing it to be channelled forth demands continuous grounding, self-awareness, self-acceptance and self-love. You can only fully perform your role as an Oracle if you have undertaken the hard work of Shadow Work. Shadow Work prepares and initiates you into this new realm of being a bringer of light.

Once you start listening to and channelling the subtle messages of the soul, you are transformed. And the more you do it, and the more adept and confident you become, the more you will enjoy the sacred duty of transmitting the words from beyond your conscious mind.

It is my sincere hope that you have relished and cherished this journey towards unifying yourself to become the Oracle.

Remember that when you become the Oracle, you are both the message and the messenger. You are sacred. You are divine. You are magnificent.

May you bring light and love to yourself and others as you become whole.

Nikki xx

AN INVITATION TO SHARE

Dear Shadow Worker

You're now at the end of my book and I hope you're enjoying reading it as much as I loved writing it.

As you know from my story at the beginning of this book, I've gone through many of the challenges you have on your Shadow Work journey. My mission has been to share information and wisdom and empower people like you. Everything I do is aligned with this value.

I'd like to invite you to jump on board with me and my mission to empower people by leaving a review for this book. Your gift won't cost you any money and will take less than 60 seconds of your time, but in giving this gift, you'll be sharing what you've learned with someone else.

[Insert QR Code here]

May the blessings flow to you from this gift of sharing.

Nikki

www.go2gurupublishing.com

Go2Guru
PUBLISHING

ABOUT THE AUTHOR

Coming from a family of lawyers, Nikki Goldstein bucked the trend and became a journalist. Despite journalism being a perfectly respectable profession, her father never stopped worrying about her or being suspicious of journalists. To prove to him she could make a "proper" living, she wrote 11 books and was an awarded copywriter and journalist. It didn't help. Her Dad was still worried.

Nikki began her career at Vogue and went on to hold senior editorial positions at Elle and Marie-Claire. She's well known for ***GirlForce***, a teen girl self-empowerment series of seven books. The series was published in the USA, Russia, Israel and Greece. In 2004 ***GirlForce*** won a prestigious Australian Publishing Association award, the Random House Best Designed Children's Series.

With a passion for helping people be their best selves, and ignoring her parent's worst fears, Nikki has studied counselling and Jungian studies (heaven knows she needed to).

When she's not working on her publishing business, Go2Guru, she's attending to her two needy dachshunds, Archie and Sunny, or doing yoga on her deck in Sydney.

RESOURCES

https://www.amazon.com.au/Women-Who-Run-Wolves/dp/1846041090/ref=asc_df_1846041090/

https://nathanielbranden.com/sentence-completion-i/#:.

Marion Woodman (2001). "Coming Home to Myself: Reflections for Nurturing a Woman's Body and Soul", p.93, Conari Press

https://www.goodreads.com/book/show/9357632-works-by-carl-jung-study-guide?ac=1&from_search=true&qid=00kPwZOXS4&rank=1

https://www.amazon.com.au/RETURN-LOVE-REFLECTIONS-Reflections-Principles/dp/0060927488

https://www.amazon.com.au/Collected-Works-C-G-Jung-Psychology/dp/0691097720

https://www.goodreads.com/book/show/144606.Border_of_a_Dream

https://www.ncbi.nlm.nih.gov/pmc/articles/PMC4814782/

https://academic.oup.com/scan/article/15/10/1086/5815969

https://www.medicalnewstoday.com/articles/320368#how-does-it-work

https://hbr.org/2022/04/the-power-of-natural-language-processing

https://www.smh.com.au/technology/unsw-researchers-find-human-intuition-does-exist-20160415-go7ii8.html

https://www.amazon.com.au/Hero-Thousand-faces-Joseph-Campbell/dp/1577315936/ref=asc_df_1577315936/

Jung, C. G. (1953). Collected Works of C.G. Jung, Volume 9 (Part 1): Archetypes and the Collective Unconscious. Princeton University Press.

Jung, C. G. (1968). Collected Works of C.G. Jung, Volume 7: Two Essays on Analytical Psychology. Princeton University Press.

Shamdasani, S. (2009). Introduction to Jungian Psychology: Notes of the Seminar on Analytical Psychology Given in 1925. Princeton University Press.

https://www.researchgate.net/publication/265165687_Measuring_Intuition_Unconscious_Emotional_Information_Boost_Decision-Making_Accuracy_and_Confidence

https://www.unsw.edu.au/newsroom/news/2024/02/what-is-a-gut-feeling-and-when-should-you-listen-to-it

https://www.amazon.com.au/Greatest-Miracle-World-Og-Mandino/dp/0553279726#:.

https://positivepsychology.com/attachment-theory/

https://www.ncbi.nlm.nih.gov/pmc/articles/PMC3051370/

https://www.goodreads.com/quotes/400367-there-is-strong-shadow-where-there-is-much-light

https://www.researchgate.net/publication/333099626_The_Effect_of_Expressive_Writing_on_Symptoms_of_Depression_in_College_Students_Randomized_Controlled_Trial

Smyth, J. M., Hockemeyer, J. R., & Tulloch, H. (2019). Expressive writing and health: Self-regulation of emotion-related experience, physiology, and behavior. Health Psychology, 38(12), 1180–1190.

Pennebaker, J. W., & Beall, S. K. (2018). Confronting a traumatic event: Toward an understanding of inhibition and disease. Annual Review of Clinical Psychology, 14, 209–235.

Frattaroli, J. (2006). Experimental disclosure and its moderators: A meta-analysis. Psychological Bulletin, 132(6), 823–865.

https://www.va.gov/WHOLEHEALTHLIBRARY/docs/Therapeutic-Journaling.pdf

https://www.amazon.com/Aion-Researches-Phenomenology-Collected-Works/dp/069101826X/ref=sr_1_1?keywords=jung+aion&qid=1585402061&sr=8-1

https://jonkabat-zinn.com/

https://www.clarendonhousebooks.com/single-post/the-wisdom-of-jung

https://www.feminist.com/resources/artspeech/genwom/conscious.html

https://www.goodreads.com/book/show/9544.Owning_Your_Own_Shadow

https://www.oxfordreference.com/display/10.1093/acref/9780191866692.001.0001/q-oro-ed6-00007024#

https://www.oxfordreference.com/display/10.1093/acref/9780191866692.001.0001/q-oro-ed6-00007024#:.

https://www.amazon.co.uk/Soul-Rumi-Coleman-Barks/dp/0060604522